T0330664

Death and Funeral Practices in Japan

This book provides a clear and comprehensive introduction to the past, present, and future direction of death rituals and deathcare systems within Japan.

As Japan heads toward a precarious future shaped by its super-ageing society, secularisation, and economic stagnation, the socioreligious structures that once organised death and funeral practice are becoming increasingly unstable. In their place, new social structures, technologies, and rituals for the farewell of the dead, handling of cremains, and commemoration of the ancestors have begun to emerge. The work is informed by the authors' extensive research within Japan's funeral, cemetery, and memorialisation sectors and the latest Japanese data sources and academic publications, many of which are not currently available in English.

Providing readily accessible and contextualising information, this book will be an essential reference for graduate students and academics, as well as international policymakers and deathcare practitioners.

Hannah Gould is a Cultural Anthropologist working in the areas of death, religion, and material culture, with a regional specialisation in Australia and North-East Asia.

Aki Miyazawa is a Sociologist of Religion working in the areas of death and funerary practices in contemporary societies.

Shinya Yamada is Professor of Folkloristics at the National Museum of Japanese History and a world-leading expert on death and funerals in Japan.

Routledge International Focus on Death and Funeral Practices

Series Editor: **Julie Rugg**, *University of York, UK*

Death Studies is an international and interdisciplinary endeavour and encompasses an interest in all mortality-related themes. This series of shortform books provides essential information on death and funeral practices in countries throughout the world.

Fully referenced, and supported by relevant images, figures and tables, books in the series provide an essential research resource on practices, the law, and funeral-related procedures around the world. Collectively, the series provides an invaluable framework for international comparison.

This series is a continuation of *Funerary International*, a series distributed by Emerald Publishing. Four books were published in this legacy series: *Funerary Practices in England and Wales* (Rugg & Parsons, 2018); *Funerary Practices in the Netherlands* (Mathijssen & Venhorst, 2019); *Funerary Practices in the Czech Republic* (Nešporová, 2021); and *Funerary Practices in Serbia* (Pavićević, 2021).

Death and Funeral Practices in Portugal
Rafaela Ferraz Ferreira, Ana Júlia Almeida Miranda and Francisco Queiroz

Death and Funeral Practices in Poland
Edited by Anna E. Kubiak, Anna Długozima and Agnieszka Wedeł-Domaradzka

Death and Funeral Practices in Japan
Hannah Gould, Aki Miyazawa, and Shinya Yamada

For more information on the series please visit: www.routledge.com/Routledge-International-Focus-on-Death-and-Funeral-Practices/book-series/DEATH

Death and Funeral Practices in Japan

Hannah Gould, Aki Miyazawa, and Shinya Yamada

LONDON AND NEW YORK

First published 2025
by Routledge
4 Park Square, Milton Park, Abingdon, Oxon OX14 4RN

and by Routledge
605 Third Avenue, New York, NY 10158

Routledge is an imprint of the Taylor & Francis Group, an informa business

© 2025 Hannah Gould, Aki Miyazawa, and Shinya Yamada

The right of Hannah Gould, Aki Miyazawa, and Shinya Yamada to be identified
as authors of this work has been asserted in accordance with sections 77 and 78
of the Copyright, Designs and Patents Act 1988.

All rights reserved. No part of this book may be reprinted or reproduced or utilised
in any form or by any electronic, mechanical, or other means, now known or
hereafter invented, including photocopying and recording, or in any information
storage or retrieval system, without permission in writing from the publishers.

Trademark notice: Product or corporate names may be trademarks or registered trademarks,
and are used only for identification and explanation without intent to infringe.

British Library Cataloguing-in-Publication Data
A catalogue record for this book is available from the British Library

Library of Congress Cataloging-in-Publication Data
Names: Gould, Hannah (Anthropologist), author. | Miyazawa, Aki, author. |
Yamada, Shinya, 1968– author.
Title: Death and funeral practices in Japan / Hannah Gould,
Aki Miyazawa and Shinya Yamada.
Description: First edition. | New York : Routledge, 2025. |
Series: Routledge international focus on death and funeral practices |
Includes bibliographical references and index.
Identifiers: LCCN 2024018345 (print) | LCCN 2024018346 (ebook) |
ISBN 9781032588742 (hbk) | ISBN 9781032588759 (pbk) |
ISBN 9781003451914 (ebk)
Subjects: LCSH: Funeral rites and ceremonies–Japan–History. |
Death care industry–Japan. | Death–Japan–Religious aspects. |
Japan–History. | Japan–Religious life and customs. |
Japan–Social life and customs.
Classification: LCC GT3284.A2 .G678 2025 (print) |
LCC GT3284.A2 (ebook) | DDC 393.0952–dc23/eng/20240606
LC record available at https://lccn.loc.gov/2024018345
LC ebook record available at https://lccn.loc.gov/2024018346

ISBN: 9781032588742 (hbk)
ISBN: 9781032588759 (pbk)
ISBN: 9781003451914 (ebk)

DOI: 10.4324/9781003451914

Typeset in Times New Roman
by Newgen Publishing UK

Contents

Textual Conventions

Japanese names are presented family name first, with the exception of authors publishing in English.

All translations are by the authors unless otherwise stated. The modified Hepburn system for the romanisation of Japanese is used throughout.

Japanese loan words are the same in singular and plural form, thus "one *tsunami*" or "many *tsunami*".

Acknowledgements

This book is indebted to the extraordinary wealth of original research that has been conducted into Japanese death and funeral practices by numerous scholars across many decades. Much of this work has never been translated into English, and as such, is often overlooked or ignored by death studies scholars, social scientists, and others working in the field. Our intention with *Death and Funeral Practices in Japan* is to increase visibility and access to this research, and to inspire a new generation of bilingual scholarship on these topics. Further, we hope that this book serves as a reminder of the benefits of multilingual scholarship and international collaboration, as well as the need to look outside the Anglosphere when seeking to theorise dying, death, and bereavement.

One particular challenge we encountered when writing this book was the translation of Japanese terminology into English, particularly with regard to unique cultural festivals, objects, and religious terms. In this endeavour, the authors would like to thank the following scholars for their expert advice: Dana Mirsalis, Takei Kengo, and Toishiba Shiho.

We would also like to acknowledge the experts and organisations that provided data sets and images: Gwyn McClelland, Nishiyama Tetsuo of Hōsenji, Sumida Kōtarō of Shūkyō Kōgeisha, Butsudan no Hasegawa, and the Ending Centre.

This work additionally draws on ethnographic fieldwork conducted by Hannah Gould with funding from the Japan Foundation Fellowship (2017).

The authors would like to thank the series editor for *Routledge International Focus on Death and Funeral Practices*, Julie Rugg, for instigating this wonderful series, and for her insightful comments and support throughout the process. Our gratitude, also, to the editorial team at Routledge for their attentiveness and encouragement.

1 Japan

An Introduction

Japan, *Nihon* or *Nippon* (日本), is a country located in North-East Asia. Japan is an archipelago, consisting of over 14,000 islands. This includes the four largest islands of Hokkaidō, Honshū, Shikoku, and Kyūshū, which together comprise mainland Japan (Figure 1.1). Honshū is the largest island and contains Tokyo, the capital city and modern seat of parliament, as well as the major cities of Osaka and Nagoya, and Kyoto, the historic capital and centre of religious life.

According to the Statistics Bureau of Japan, the contemporary population of Japan is 124.34 million people.[1] This makes Japan the 11th most populated nation state. As approximately 75% of the country's terrain is covered by forested mountains, the population is densely concentrated in narrow coastal plains. As of 2021, about 92% of the Japanese population reside in cities.[2] The capital city Tokyo is part of the Greater Tokyo Area, which is the largest metropolitan area in the world, with over 40 million residents.[3]

The archipelago of Japan is located along the Pacific Ring of Fire, a massive tectonic belt that circumscribes the Pacific Ocean. Given this position, Japan is vulnerable to natural disasters, including volcanoes, typhoons, earthquakes, and tsunami. Major earthquakes of the modern era, including in Kantō in 1923, Hanshin in 1995, and Tōhoku in 2011, have led to mass death events.

Japan is a modern democracy, governed through a constitutional monarchy, with a two-house parliament. The country is divided into 47 administrative prefectures. The Imperial Household of Japan, headed by the Emperor, is the oldest continuing hereditary monarchy in the world. According to Article 1 of the post-WWII constitution, the Emperor is "the symbol of the State and of the unity of the people"[4] but has no direct power and no role in the affairs of government.

DOI: 10.4324/9781003451914-1

Figure 1.1   Map of Japan. Licensed image (Contributor: Peter Hermes Furian).

Archaeological evidence suggests that the Japanese archipelago has been inhabited since the Paleolithic Era by the Jōmon people. This population mixed with ethnic groups (the Yayoi people) that subsequently migrated from the East Asian mainland. Prominent events in the early history of Japan include the 'golden age' of classical Japanese culture under the Heian Court and Imperial Rule in the 8th century, and periods of civil war between rival shogunates (hereditary military dictatorships) in the 14th and 15th centuries. Japan was unified in the late 16th and early 17th century under the leadership of Oda Nobunaga, Toyotomi Hideyoshi, and the Tokugawa Shogunate.

Until the Edo period, eras of Japanese history were typically named after the centre of political power at the time. Since the 19th century, when the Emperor system was restored, it has become common to use the imperial name or *gengō* to refer to eras (Table 1.1). For example, 2025 is Reiwa 7. The financial year in Japan runs between 1 April and the 31 March, with official statistics reported within this period.

This book focuses on contemporary Japan, while giving the context required for readers to understand the deep histories of Japanese

Table 1.1 Table of Japanese historical periods with corresponding dates in the Gregorian calendar

Japanese Historical Period	Years in the Gregorian Calendar
Asuka	538–710
Nara	710–794
Heian	794–1185
Kamakura	1185–1333
Muromachi	1333–1573
Edo or Tokugawa	1600–1867
Meiji	1868–1912
Taishō	1912–1926
Shōwa	1926–1989
Heisei	1989–2019
Reiwa	2019–

death and funeral practices. The modern era of Japan began with the Meiji Restoration of 1868, which returned Japan to imperial rule and led to widespread social and political changes, including the opening of Japan to Western trade, rapid industrialisation, and social liberalisation. This is also arguably when popular consciousness of a unified Japanese ethnicity and nation state was formed.

Modern Japanese history is marked by its participation and subsequent defeat in WWII, in the wake of atomic bombs being dropped on Nagasaki and Hiroshima. The war resulted in American occupation and a new constitution that stripped the Emperor of their powers and enforced pacifism. The Japanese economy rapidly grew post-war, bringing millions into the middle class, until the economic bubble burst in the market crash of the early 1990s. Today, Japan remains a global powerhouse in manufacturing and technology; however it faces significant challenges in the form of economic stagnation, an ageing population, and a falling birth rate.

Contemporary Japan is an ethnically and culturally homogenous society, with Japanese people comprising 98.1% of the country's population.[5] Minority ethnic populations include Indigenous peoples, such as the Ainu and Ryukyuan peoples, as well as migrant communities, notably, Koreans, Chinese, and Brazilians. Those born overseas make up a growing percentage of the total population. This book focuses on death and funeral practices of the ethnic Japanese majority, while noting the significant cultural and regional differences that do exist.

Most Japanese people are affiliated with one or both of the country's two major religions: Buddhism and Shintoism. However, the vast majority identify as non-religious and participate in religion as a cultural practice.[6] Buddhism came to Japan in the 6th century and spread rapidly as the religion of the ruling classes and funeral rites. Folk religious practices have existed since the earliest inhabitation of the archipelago, often mixing with Buddhism, Confucianism, and other influences. Shintoism derives from these folk practices and came to be codified as a distinct religion in the modern period. It is also the religion of the modern Imperial Household. The vast majority of funerals in Japan are Buddhist, but services for deceased Emperors in the modern era are conducted with Shinto rites.

Notes

1 Statistics Bureau of Japan 総務省統計局, "人口推計（2022年（令和4年）10月1日現在全国：年齢（各歳）、男女別人口・都道府県：年齢（5歳階級）、男女別人口-", April 4, 2023, www.stat.go.jp/data/jinsui/2022np/index.html.
2 Statistica, "Japan: Degree of urbanization from 2011 to 2021," May, 2023, www.statista.com/statistics/270086/urbanization-in-japan/#:~:text=In%20the%20past%20decade%2C%20Japan's,off%20at%20around%2091.9%20percent.
3 Ministry of Land, Infrastructure, Transport and Tourism 国土交通省, "首都圏整備の状況," Vol. 2, 2015, www.mlit.go.jp/common/001131242.pdf.
4 The Constitution of Japan, *Prime Minister of Japan and His Cabinet*, accessed January 12, 2024, https://japan.kantei.go.jp/constitution_and_government_of_japan/constitution_e.html.
5 Chris Burgess, "Multicultural Japan?," *The Asia-Pacific Journal* 5, no. 3 (March 2007).
6 Kobayashi Toshiyuki 小林利行, "日本人の宗教的意識や行動はどう変わったか," *NHK Broadcasting Research and Surveys*, April 2019, www.nhk.or.jp/bunken/research/yoron/pdf/20190401_7.pdf.

2 History

In contemporary Japan, the overwhelming majority of funerals are conducted with the participation of a Buddhist priest, followed by families interring cremated remains in multi-generational graves. However, this system has undergone seismic shifts in the past, closely linked to changes in social conditions and political systems, as well as people's changing views of life and death.

2.1 From Ancient Times to the Advent of Buddhism

The introduction of Buddhism did not immediately lead to the spread of Buddhist funeral rites across Japan. Buddhism first came to Japan via the Korean peninsula in the 6th century, when political power was centred in the Kinai region (around contemporary Nara). With the centralisation of government authority during the Asuka (592–710) and Nara periods (710–794), Buddhism became established as the religion of the ruling class. From this time, Buddhist rites were performed at the time of the death of emperors and nobles. Those upper classes who could afford to construct tombs were buried within them, while the bodies of common people were disposed of via excarnation (open exposure to nature).[1] There is some evidence that some wealthy peasants also built tombs in ancient times.[2]

During this period, Buddhist officials were exclusively engaged in state rituals for emperors and nobles, not commoners. There was also a strong belief at the time regarding the pollution of death. In the ancient code of laws and customs, *Engishiki* (延喜式), of 927, death was considered the most polluting force, requiring various rites to purify the defilement, such as a period of vegetarianism and

DOI: 10.4324/9781003451914-2

abstinence. Buddhist priests engaged in state rituals (官僧 *kansō*)[3] were obliged to avoid the pollution generated by the death of common folk so as not to interfere with their other sacred duties.[4]

The first official record of a cremation taking place in Japan is of Buddhist priest Dōshō (道昭), who was cremated as per his dying wish in the year 700.[5] Priests of this era saw cremation as a particularly meritorious path toward enlightenment in emulation of the founder of Buddhism, Śākyamuni Buddha.[6] In 704, Emperor Jitō became the first emperor to be cremated, and this practice was rapidly accepted amongst the Japanese populace in the period thereafter.

The spread of cremation was not simply the result of Buddhism's influence. Other influences in cremation's early adoption include administrative restructuring, the social hygiene movement, and the Funeral Simplification Order (薄葬令 *hakusōrei*), which was issued by the Imperial Household in 646 as part of a broad slate of social reforms, known as the Taika Reforms (大化の改新 *taika no kaishin*).[7] The Funeral Simplification Order restricted the size and elaborateness of graves that could be constructed for all. This order saw the end of the ancient practice of constructing monumental keyhole-shaped burial mounds, known as *kofun* (古墳), for nobles in Japan.

2.2 Buddhist Rites in the Medieval to Early Modern Period

In the medieval period (c. 1185–1603), warrior classes begun to amass military and then political power, leading to major changes in the social order. During these turbulent times, growing popular interest emerged in ideas of a Buddhist afterlife, which also had a vast impact on Japanese funerary customs.

The 11th century saw the spread of popular belief in the existence of a Buddhist Pure Land (浄土 *jōdo*), being the paradise that believers travel to when they die.[8] In 986, Genshin (源信, 942–1017) formed a mutual association (二十五三昧会 *nijūgo-zanmaie*) comprised of 25 priests who agreed to assist each other with funerals so as to prevent their bodies from being abandoned after their death. The association cared for dying members, transported and buried their remains, and chanted sutras throughout the night to deliver the dead to the Pure Land. This model was revolutionary at the time, and when it spread to general society in the late 13th century, it ended the practice of excarnation.[9] In the late 12th to 13th centuries burial grounds began to be established around the country as these associations gradually opened to lay people. People also started burying human remains at Buddhist sacred sites so as to deliver the spirit of the dead to the Pure Land, where previously, these sites were only visited by living pilgrims.[10]

Genshin's mutual association was pioneering in that it disavowed the pollution of death. Even more radically, during the Kamakura period (1185–1333), a group of priests actively involved in funerals began to emerge. They established the culture of death that continues in Japan today. These so-called "seclusion priests" (遁世僧 *tonseisō*) renounced their status as imperial court officials in order to bring salvation to the common people. Their role in funeral rites won them favour in Japanese society.[11] In particular, Zen Buddhism was one of the first to introduce its model of funeral rites for deceased priests, the *Motsugo-Sasō* (没後作僧), to its lay followers. Zen's proclivity toward funerary rites contributed to its popularity among the general population during the medieval period. The *Motsugo-Sasō* became the prototype for Buddhist funerals in Japan. Many funerary goods used in Japan until modern times, such as the *gan* (龕 palanquin transporting a coffin), *zakan* (座棺 seated coffin), and *shika* (四花 paper flowers), were also developed in Zen Buddhism[12].

The Edo Shogunate ruled for a span of over 300 years. Via the religious control exercised by the government, the relationship between Buddhism and funerals solidified. Between the 15th and 17th centuries, Japan's manorial system of land ownership and governance collapsed amidst repeated wars, and self-governing villages were formed in each region. Buddhism took root in these local communities, each of which established a temple as the centre for funeral rites. Most present-day temples were built during this period of about 200 years, between 1467 to 1665.[13]

Based on these budding ties between temples and the people, the Shogunate introduced the temple certification system (寺請制度 *terauke seido*) in the 17th century. This system aimed to eliminate the growing influence of Christianity, which arrived in Japan a century earlier. Temple certification made Buddhist priests the guarantors of the status of their parishioners (檀家 *danka*) as (mainstream) Buddhists, and not as a follower of a foreign religion or radical Buddhist school.[14] Every person was obligated to belong to a Buddhist temple, and temples were given the exclusive right to conduct funerals for their parishioners in return for their role in governance and administration.

2.3 The Modernisation of Funerary Practices in Japan

The rule of the Tokugawa Shogunate ended with the political upheaval of the Meiji Restoration in 1868, which propelled Japan toward becoming a modern, industrial nation-state. In short, the Meiji Restoration removed the Tokugawa Shogun and his feudal lords from power and returned the Emperor to centralised rule over Japan. This event also represents the beginning of significant foreign influence in Japan after the isolationist Tokugawa period. Under the new government, modern ideas of industry, education, and sanitation were introduced, and a new legal system was adopted, furnishing the basic framework of deathcare infrastructure that continues today.

The new government enacted policies to weaken the power of Buddhist temples by implementing Shinto nationalism. In particular, they promoted Shinto funeral rites. Shintoism is the traditional, broadly animist, religion of Japan, that centres around living harmoniously with the spirit world (Chapter 5). Before the Meiji Restoration, there was a high degree of syncretism between Buddhism and Shintoism. The Meiji Government issued the Shinto-Buddhist Separation Order (神仏分離令 *shinbutsu bunrirei*) in 1868, and in the same year, Shinto funeral rites, which until then had in principle only been permitted for the Shinto priesthood, were also permitted for priests' family members.[15] In 1871, the Registration Act was enacted to replace the Buddhist temple registration system, such that the state, rather than temples, came to administer the people. But this radical realignment of religious control proved unsuccessful. The promotion of Shinto funeral rites ended after only a few short years, along with a major shift in the Meiji Government's religious policy, which abandoned national Shintoism in favour of (in principle) freedom of religion.

2.3.1 Modern Cremation

Until the early Meiji period (late 1870s), burial was the dominant form of body disposal practiced in Japan, although cremation was practiced in urban areas like Tokyo, Osaka, and Kyoto, and in areas with many followers of Pure Land Buddhism, such as the Hokuriku region. In most examples of early cremation, bodies were cremated on wood-burning pyres and the bones were collected and then buried, although there were considerable regional differences.[16]

Under these circumstances, in 1873, at a time when Shintoism was being promoted as the national religion, the Meiji Government issued a nationwide ban on cremation, labelling it a "barbarian custom" of Buddhists.[17] There was much public debate about this sudden ban, and it was lifted only two years later due to a shortage of burial sites in urban centres, and due to the fact that cremation was simultaneously being promoted as the more modern, sanitary method of disposal in the West. This reversal contributed to setbacks in Shinto nationalisation policy around the same time.[18]

Subsequently, cremation was disentangled from religious issues and promoted as a hygienic practice. After the ban was lifted, the government issued Cremation Site Management Regulations (焼場取扱心得 *yakiba toriatsukai kokoroe*) to regulate the smoke emissions and odours caused by cremation and to control the establishment of new crematoria. In 1897, the government enacted the Contagious Disease Prevention Act (伝染病予防法 *densenbyō yobō hō*), which enforced the quarantine of the bodies of patients with contagious diseases and stipulated that such bodies should be cremated.[19] This further spread the practice of cremation, even to areas where burial was the norm.

2.3.2 Modern Cemeteries

The early Meiji Government (c. 1870s), hoping to promote national Shinto, was eager to secure cemeteries for Shinto burial rites. At the same time, it regarded pre-modern graveyards as a problem because they were segregated by social class, with the graves of the lower classes often poorly made and unmarked. Thus, this new reformist government aimed to establish a new grave system appropriate to a modern state.

Before this time, most graveyards, especially in Tokyo, were located within Buddhist temple precincts. In the early 1870s, the government established several new cemeteries for people receiving Shinto funeral rites and placed these cemeteries under the control of Shinto shrines. Later, in 1874, new regulations set out that all cemeteries should be authorised by the government, a principle that continues to this day.[20] However, the policy of Shinto nationalisation was soon discontinued and with it, Shinto cemeteries. From this point onwards, the government moved towards the construction of public cemeteries or *kyōsō bochi* (共葬墓地).

The establishment of *kyōsō bochi* marked the secularisation of Japan's cemetery administration and the birth of modern public cemeteries in Japan.[21] *Kyōsō bochi* accept interments of people regardless of religion, class, or place of birth. Shinto cemeteries originally established under the Shinto nationalisation policy gradually lost their religious character, and their management was transferred to local authorities between 1874 and 1876. In 1878, the Cemetery Restriction Decree (墓地制限令 *bochi seigen rei*) clarified that all funerary matters were "at the discretion of each individual" and stipulated that from 1882, all new or expanded cemeteries should be public.[22]

The culmination of modern cemetery legislation was the Cemetery and Burial Control Regulations (墓地及埋葬取締規則 *bochi oyobi maisō torishimari kisoku*) of 1884. This administered cemeteries as public health institutions rather than religious institutions, stipulated that cemeteries and crematoria could only be operated with a permit, and stipulated that bodies must not be buried or cremated within 24 hours of death.[23] Thus, body disposal practices, which had been very diverse until the early modern period, came to be administered under a single framework.

While graves came under state administration, the state did not assume responsibility for their maintenance and management. The Meiji Government defined graves as the ritual property of the household (家 *ie*) and institutionalised responsibility for them by the household. Put simply, the Meiji Civil Code, which came into force in 1898, made the care of graves the duty of the household heir. This civil code was based on the Meiji government's ideology of the family state (家族国家観 *kazoku kokka kan*), which described each Japanese household as a branch of the Emperor's household, and framed ancestral rituals and graves as the spiritual mainstay of a national family.[24]

In 1923, the Great Kantō Earthquake ravaged the area surrounding Tokyo, destroying many graves and displacing remains.[25] In response, a new grave design with underground vaults that could accommodate entire sets of household remains beneath a tombstone became popular. This design diffused throughout the country in the early 20th century (Chapter 11).

2.3.3 Modern Funerals

While the circumstances surrounding cemeteries and disposal experienced great changes in the early Meiji period, funeral practice basically remained consistent. A funeral procession (葬列 *sōrestu*) from the home to the temple or graveyard, where the ceremony was held, was particularly important as a ritual to convey the dead to the afterlife. Processions were also a means of marking attendees' familial and social status, by allocating them each a distinct role (such as carrying the coffin or mortuary tablet). For example, only male relatives carried objects, while women followed in rickshaws.[26] From the Meiji period onwards, the funeral procession became more flamboyant, as people who had been restricted in funeral displays under the strict status system of the Edo Shogunate begun to display flowers or release birds[27] (Chapter 6). Funerals were carried out by relatives and neighbours of the deceased, and there were many rituals that brought people into direct contact with the dead body, such as washing and encoffining.

Although extravagant funeral processions had been criticised by intellectuals during the Meiji period, it was not until the Taisho period (1912–1926) that the custom of processions came to an end. In Tokyo, the development of railways and other transport networks made it impossible to hold large funeral processions and people lost the custom of walking long distances, resulting in fewer attendees on foot. The Cemetery and Burial Control Regulations prohibited burial in urban areas and all crematoria were located outside the city, meaning that people had to travel longer distances to funerals.[28] With the end of processions, hearses began to be used in urban areas.[29]

Instead of the funeral procession, a farewell ceremony (告別式 *kokubetsushiki*) became the focal point of funeral rites. The first documented farewell ceremony in Japan was that of the social thinker and politician Nakae Chōmin (中江兆民, 1847–1901). Nakae rejected religious rites and left a will asking for no funeral at all. However, his family and friends wanted a funeral and eventually held a non-religious ceremony called *kokubetsushiki*. The ceremony consisted mainly of eulogies, speeches, and other acts of condolence and farewell. It was a ritual that removed religious elements from traditional funeral rites.[30] Later, during the Taishō era (1912–1926), this farewell ceremony became popular among intelligentsia who were critical of traditional funerals. However, unlike the non-religious funeral of Nakae, many *kokubetushiki* were combined with more religious rituals, such as the burning of incense (焼香 *shōkō*). By the end of the Taishō era, home farewell ceremonies, held at the bereaved's residence, became more common. In this manner, with the disappearance of the funeral procession, funerals became less public community events and more private household events.

The funeral industry also underwent significant changes during this period. Funeral arrangers, who lost significant revenue with the end of funeral processions, began diversifying to take on other labours such as encoffining and registering deaths. As home ceremonies became more popular, it became common to display a temporary funeral altar in the home. These altars became signs of social status and provided opportunities for the expansion of funeral arrangers' business.[31] Specialist professionals, such as funeral directors and crematorium staff began to play a greater role in funeral activity.

2.4 Post-war to the Present

The Second World War was a mass-death event for Japan, with significant losses of both armed forces and civilians. The most acute, violent deaths were caused by the 1945 atomic bombings of Nagasaki and Hiroshima, which together killed between 110,000 and 210,000 persons.[32] In the immediate wake of these atrocities, emergency measures were put in place to handle the deceased, including mass cremations and funerals.

After the deaths and devastation of the Second World War, Japan was re-launched as a new democratic state under the direction of the United States and Allied Powers. State Shinto was demolished, and the feudalistic pre-war constitution and Meiji civil code were rewritten. After years of economic depression, people's lives became rapidly more affluent as Japan entered a period of rapid growth in the 1960s. The way people died changed dramatically along with their lifestyles.

One of the major changes of the post-war period was a decline in mortality rates and increased longevity. This was brought about by developments in public health, advances in medical technology, improved standards of living, and the introduction of public health insurance. In 1947, life expectancy was 50.06 years for men and 53.96 for women; by 2010 it had increased dramatically to 79.64 years for men and 86.39 for women respectively, making Japan one of the longest-living countries in the world.[33] Curbing the spread of infectious diseases was a major factor in declining mortality. In 1947, tuberculosis was the leading cause of death, followed by pneumonia and bronchitis in second, and gastroenteritis in third. However, by 2021, cancer was the leading cause of death, followed by heart disease and senility.[34] Younger people (including infants) are no longer dying suddenly from infectious diseases. As of 2019, deaths of people aged 75 and over accounted for 76.5% of all deaths in Japan.[35]

In the past, it was common for people to draw their final breaths at home, watched over by their family and community, but in recent years, the vast majority die in hospital. In 1951, 82.5% of deaths occurred at home. Deaths in institutions (hospitals, medical clinic, etc.) first surpassed home deaths in the 1970s, and by 2005, a mere 12.2% of deaths occurred at home.[36] Today there is a trend towards respecting the wishes of the dying person and advanced care planning, and the dominance of hospital death may be slowly reversing. Broader post-war welfare reforms include the introduction of the Public Assistance Act (1950) and National Funeral Assistance (Chapter 8).

A nationwide shift to cremation is also a feature of the post-war period. Although there were significant regional differences, the national cremation rate rose from 43.2% in 1925 to surpass burial in 1940, at 55.7%. By 1980, the national cremation rate had risen to 91.1%.[37] This increase is linked to the pre-war promotion of cremation from the perspective of public health and city planning, and to the proliferation of public crematoria in multiple regions after the war. Along with the establishment of permanent public crematoria, deteriorating cremation facilities, such as open-air pyres, were gradually abolished. Cremation came to be carried out in specialised facilities operated by professionals.

While people's lifestyles have changed significantly, the pre-war style of funeral rites continued for some time after the war. For example, household graves continued to be inherited by the head of the household (usually the eldest son) in accordance with traditional custom, despite the fact that the old civil code was amended post-war.[38] Furthermore, in 1946, immediately after the war, regulations around the opening of new cemeteries eased, making it possible for the private sector to create cemeteries. New urbanites during this period of rapid economic growth needed graves. Urbanisation led to the deterioration of connections between households and their family temple (菩提寺 *bodaijii*), and so families begun to purchase graves in private (secular) cemeteries.[39]

With regard to funerals, the structure of the funeral rite formally maintained pre-war patterns, although ritual knowledge, as well as the capacity and resources to organise funerals, shifted to professionals.[40] In urban areas, the village was replaced by the company as the key social unit and the modern profession of 'funeral director' emerged.[41] Japanese companies of the post-war period fostered a communal spirit through a lifetime employment system and provision of housing and healthcare. Many companies thus also became involved in organising their employees' funerals. The number of attendees at funerals in the post-war period increased, expanding to include personal friends and colleagues. In recent decades, these large funerals have become a burden on families financially and socially, leading to criticism of the funeral industry[42] (Chapter 7).

When Japan's bubble economy burst in the 1990s and the country fell into a sudden recession, social inequalities were exposed. Household graves, which were established on the premise of succession by descendants, proved difficult to maintain in perpetuity as the number of children declined. Thus, from the 1990s onwards, several options for the interment of cremated remains that do not require succession began to appear, including ash scattering, tree burial, communal graves, and ossuaries. Economic recession and a rising average age of mortality has seen a marked trend towards smaller funeral services. This trend was accelerated by Covid-19. In Japan, a state of emergency was first declared on 7 April 2020, and an atmosphere of restraint associated with social gatherings led to an increase in smaller funerals. According to a survey conducted by Kamakura Shinsho, conventional funerals (一般葬 *ippansō*) which are usually attended by acquaintances, accounted for 48.9% of all funerals before Covid-19, but during the pandemic, this decreased to 25.9%. Conversely, smaller funerals attended only by close family become the majority, at 55.7%.[43] Including the aforementioned pandemic, various major events have further shaped death and funeral practices in the post-2000s period, including most notably, the March 2011 earthquake and tsunami.

Notes

1 Katsuda Itaru 勝田至, *死者たちの中世* (東京: 吉川弘文館, 2003).
2 Katsuda Itaru 勝田至, ed., *日本葬制史* (東京: 吉川弘文館, 2012), 118–22.
3 In general, when discussing Japanese Buddhism, the term 'priest' (not 'monk' or 'monastic') is preferred, given that throughout history many religious officials have not, and today do not, uphold Buddhist monastic codes or *vinaya*.
4 Matsuo Kenji 松尾剛次, *葬式仏教の誕生* (東京: 平凡社, 2011), 54–7.

In the 10th century, as the syncretism of Shintoism and Buddhism progressed, imperial Buddhist priests became strongly involved in Shinto rituals, such as reciting prayers before the *kami*, which is said to have further influenced their avoidance of the pollutions of death.

5 Hayashi Ei'ichi 林英一, 近代火葬の民俗学 (京都: 法蔵館, 2010), 71–2. However, archaeological studies suggest that cremation was practiced before Dōshō's cremation.

6 Andrew Bernstein, *Modern Passings* (Honolulu: University of Hawai'i Press, 2006), 300.

7 Hayashi 林, 近代火葬の民俗学, 72–3.

8 In Buddhism there exist multiple buddhas across time and space, each residing within their own cosmic realm. Generally speaking, when Japanese Buddhists refer to the Pure Land, they refer to *Saihō Gokuraku Jōdo* (西方極楽浄土), which is the realm of Amida Buddha. Fujii Masao 藤井正雄, Hanayama Shōyū 花山勝友 and Nakano Tōzen 中野東禅, 仏教葬祭大事典 (東京: 雄山閣, 1980), 288–90.

9 Katsuda 勝田, 死者たちの中世.

10 Satō Hiro'o 佐藤弘夫, 死者のゆくえ (東京: 岩田書院, 2004).

11 Matsuo 松尾, 葬式仏教の誕生.

12 Gojokai Hoshō Kabushiki Gaisya 互助会保証株式会社 and Ippan Syadan Hōjin Zen-Nihon Kankonsōsai Gojokyōkai 一般社団法人全日本冠婚葬祭互助協会 eds., 冠婚葬祭の歴史. (東京: 水曜社, 2014), 72.

13 Tamamuro Taijō 圭室諦成, 葬式仏教 (東京: 大法輪閣, 1979), 210.

14 Houzawa Naohide 朴澤直秀, "寺檀制度と葬祭仏教," in 生と死, シリーズ日本人と宗教 近世から近代へ3, ed. Shimazono Susumu 島薗進, Takano Toshihiko 高埜利彦, Hayashi Makoto 林淳 and Wakao Masaki 若尾政希 (東京: 春秋社, 2015), 25–51.

In a narrow sense, the temple *parishioner* system is a political system, with the temple *certification* system of the Edo period at its core. However, people tend to use the term "temple parishioner system" broadly.

15 Mori Kenji 森謙二, 墓と葬送の社会史 (東京: 講談社, 1993), 136.

16 Hayashi 林, 近代火葬の民俗学, 97–113.

17 Bernstein, *Modern Passings*, 68–71.

18 Bernstein, *Modern Passings*, 300.

19 Mori Shigeru 森茂, 日本の葬送・墓地 (京都: 法律文化社, 2013), 18.

20 Mori 森, 墓と葬送の社会史, 153–4.

21 Koretsune Keisuke 此経啓助, "明治時代の文化政策と宗教政策," 日本大学芸術学部紀要 41 (2005): 43–60.

22 Toishiba Shiho 問芝志保, 先祖祭祀と墓制の近代 (神奈川: 春風社, 2020), 130–2.

23 Mori 森, 日本の葬送・墓地, 25.

The provision that no burial or cremation shall take place within 24 hours of death is also stipulated in Article 3 of the Graveyard and Burial Act. This is intended to ensure that there is no possibility of resuscitation.

24 Mori 森, 墓と葬送の社会史, 180–1.

25 Toishiba Shiho 問芝志保, "関東大震災と家族納骨墓," 宗教研究 *393* (2018): 51–74.

26 Murakami Kōkyō, "Changes in Japanese Urban Funeral Customs during the Twentieth Century," *Japanese Journal of Religious Studies* 27, no. 3–4 (Fall 2000): 338.

27 Tanaka Daisuke 田中大介, 葬儀業のエスノグラフィ (東京: 東京大学出版会, 2017).

28 Murakami Kōkyō 村上興匡, "大正期東京における葬送儀礼の変化と近代化," 宗教研究 64, no. 1 (1990): 37–61.

29 Inoue Shōichi 井上章一, 増補新版 霊柩車の誕生 (東京: 朝日新聞出版, 2013).

30 Murakami Kōkyō 村上興匡, "中江兆民の死と葬儀," 東京大学宗教学年報 19 (2001):1–14.

31 Yamada Shinya 山田慎也, 現代日本の死と葬儀 (東京: 東京大学出版会, 2007).

32 Estimating the exact total number of deaths caused by these events is difficult, given the total destruction of administrative and healthcare services caused by the atomic bombings.

33 Ministry of Health, Labour and Welfare (MHLW) 厚生労働省, 平均余命の年次推移, accessed December 18, 2023, www.mhlw.go.jp/toukei/saikin/hw/life/life10/sankou02.html.

34 MHLW 厚生労働省, 死因順位, accessed December 18, 2023, www.mhlw.go.jp/toukei/saikin/hw/jinkou/suii09/deth7.html.
According to the MHLW manual on death certificates, 'senility' is only used as a cause of death in the case of 'natural deaths' of the elderly, where no other cause of death can be found.

35 Ippanzaidanhōjin Kankonsōsai Bunka Shinkō Zaidan一般財団法人冠婚葬祭文化振興財団, 冠婚葬祭データブック, (東京: 鎌倉新書, 2021), 31.

36 MHLW, 厚生統計要覧, accessed December 18, 2023, www.mhlw.go.jp/toukei/youran/indexyk_1_2.html.
Note that until 1990, statistics for deaths in nursing homes were included in the statistics for deaths at home.

37 Seikatu Eisei Hōki Kenkyūkai 生活衛生法規研究会 ed., 新訂 逐条解説 墓地、埋葬等に関する法律 第3版（東京: 第一法規, 2007), 300–3.

38 Inoue Haruyo 井上治代, 墓と家族の変容 (東京: 岩書店, 2003).

39 Mori Kenji 森謙二, 墓と葬送の現在 (東京: 東京堂出版, 2000), 24.

40 Mark Rowe, "Stickers of Nails: The Ongoing Transformation of Roles, Rites, and Symbols in Japanese Funerals," *Japanese Journal of Religious Studies* 27 nos. 3-4 (2000): 354.

41 Hikaru Suzuki, *The Price of Death* (Stanford: Stanford University Press, 2000).

42 Katsuda 勝田, *日本葬制史*, 296–297; Gojokai Hoshō Kabushiki Gaisya 互助会保証株式会社 and Ippan Syadan Hōjin Zen-Nihon Kankonsōsai Gojokyōkai 一般社団法人全日本冠婚葬祭互助協会, *冠婚葬祭の歴史*, 83–84.

43 Kamakura Shinsho 鎌倉新書, *第5回「コロナ禍におけるお葬式の実態調査」*, accessed June 29, 2023, www.e-sogi.com/guide/46028/.

3 Governance

3.1 National Legal Frameworks

The Constitution of Japan is the highest law of the country. Below that, laws are enacted through an act of parliament (known in Japan as "the Diet"), and orders (Cabinet Orders/Ministerial Orders) that supplement the details of those laws. Within the scope of these national laws and orders, each prefectural government establishes its own ordinances. There are 47 administrative prefectures in Japan, and they contain different municipal city governments, or in the case of major metropolises, multiple ward governments.

Basic policies regarding burials, cremations, as well as the management of cemeteries, crematoria, and columbaria are outlined in the "Graveyard and Burial Act" (1948) or "GBA", and the details of its implementation are stipulated in the ministerial ordinance "Graveyard and Burial Act Enforcement Regulations" (1948). The GBA regulates the acts of burial, cremation, and reburial, as well as the establishment, management, and administration of cemeteries, columbaria, and crematoria, mainly from the perspective of public health and welfare, as well as what is described as the "religious sentiments of the people".

The GBA outlines general rules regarding cemeteries and burials, but it does not provide detailed regulations. Each prefectural government is responsible for operationalising the GBA based on their local situation and in line with other relevant statutes, such as the Building Standards Act (1950) and the City Planning Act (1968). Accordingly, prefectural governments have enacted their own sets of regulations. This does not mean that governance is entirely idiosyncratic or without general standards. In 2000, the Ministry of

DOI: 10.4324/9781003451914-3

Health and Welfare issued a notice entitled "Guidelines for Cemetery Administration and Management" (墓地経営、管理の指針等について). The documents contained in this notice give specific directives for conducting guidance and supervision work related to cemeteries. Although these directives are not legally binding, each prefectural government is instructed to refer to this document and operate accordingly.

Other national laws that regulate aspects of death and funeral practice are explored in other sections of this book. These include the Family Register Act (1947), which sets out the procedures for declaring death, issuing death certificates, and postmortem examination (Chapter 4) and the Public Assistance Act (1950), which establishes the National Funeral Assistance program (Chapter 8).

Regarding funeral companies and funeral workers, there is no qualification or licensing system currently operating in Japan, although there are various voluntary qualifications and associations (Chapter 6). Similarly, no official permission or registration is required to open a funeral business.

3.2 Local Legal Frameworks

In Japan, local governments are essentially responsible for the governance of cemeteries, crematoria, and columbaria. For example, it is the role of the Prefectural Governor to issue and cancel management permits for cemeteries, crematoria, and columbaria, as well as to instruct and supervise these facilities. If the municipality is a city or special ward, the Mayor or Head of the Ward has that authority (Article 10 of the GBA). In other prefectures these powers may be voluntarily delegated from Prefectural Governors to Municipal Mayors based on the 1947 Local Autonomy Act. Moreover, based on Article 5 of the GBA, the Municipal Mayor has a role in granting permissions for burial, cremation, and reburial.

Local governments are also responsible for guaranteeing the supply of cemetery space to residents. In fact, since 1884, from the perspective of the permanence and public interest of cemeteries, the provision of cemeteries has, in principle, been the responsibility of local governments, and the construction of new cemeteries has, in principle, been limited to these local governments. However, the supply of cemeteries by local governments is insufficient. Therefore, after World War II, religious organisations and public interest corporations have been allowed to establish new cemeteries. Today, in practice, private enterprises are responsible for guaranteeing supply.[1]

Local governments generally establish detailed rules regarding the location, construction, and amenities of cemeteries through ordinances. For example, the Tokyo Metropolitan Government requires that cemeteries are located so as not to risk contaminating drinking water, that graves be constructed of solid materials such as concrete and stone, and that a certain amount of green space be provided within cemeteries.[2] Cemeteries in Japan are a mixture of public and private (e.g. temples, private companies) ownership, and a number of privately owned graves are still in use (Chapter 10). In this context, the role of local authorities in granting licenses to operate cemeteries is becoming increasingly important.

In this manner, Japan is characterized by devolved governance of cemeteries, columbaria, and crematoria. However, this does not guarantee that local authorities will properly bury all of the dead. Historically in Japan and throughout the modern era, there has been a strong public consciousness of the household (家 *ie*), which is held responsible for disposing of the dead and conducting ancestor rites.[3] In other words, in Japan, the scope of the welfare state is not "from the cradle to the grave" but "until the moment of death", after which time the deceased is considered to be the moral responsibility of the household. If a household has difficulty obtaining or maintaining a grave (for reasons including having no successor), cremated remains may be kept temporarily in the home.[4]

3.3 Environmental Issues

Environmental considerations for cemeteries and crematoria are not mentioned in the Graveyard and Burial Act or the Graveyard and Burial Act Enforcement Regulations. Therefore, each municipality sets standards by referring to its own ordinances, and other relevant legislation (e.g. Building Standards Act, City Planning Act, etc.) and guidelines.

Historically, cemeteries and crematoria have been considered adverse amenities, akin to wholesale markets, abattoirs, and garbage incinerators,[5] and new developments have been opposed by local communities[6]. When cremation resumed *en masse* in the early Meiji Period (1868–1912), crematoria were required to be located two blocks (approximately 218 meters) away from residential areas, waterways that provide drinking water, and public roads. These restrictions have somewhat relaxed in the contemporary era but remain in place. For example, the Chiba City Ordinance[7] stipulates the following environmental standards for cemeteries:

(1) The distance from a river, sea or lake to a cemetery must be 20 metres or more;
(2) The distance from residences to a cemetery must be 100 metres or more in the case of cemeteries where whole body burial takes place, and 50 metres or more in other cases;
(3) The site where a cemetery is to be established must be on land that is not too high and dry, and is not likely to pollute drinking water; and
(4) In addition to the above items, the site where the cemetery is to be established must be on land that does not thereby pose a hazard to public health.

The ordinance also sets environmental standards for crematoria, including that (1) the distance from residences to crematoria must be 100 metres or more; and (2) the location of crematoria must be on land that does not thereby pose a hazard to public health (Article 13). With regard to facility standards, cremation furnaces must have exhaust gas re-burning equipment with sufficient capacity to prevent odour, dust, noise, and pollution from entering the atmosphere (Article 14).

In particular, the structure, equipment, and technology of crematoria have been studied by the former Ministry of Health and Welfare, as industrial pollution problems have come to the fore since Japan's period of rapid economic growth. As a result, in 1970, the Japan Centre for Environmental Health published the *Study on Crematorium Facility Standards* (火葬場の施設基準に関する研究, First Edition), which was widely used by local authorities, industry, and other stakeholders for 30 years[8]. Later, in 2000, when the control of dioxin emissions from the combustion of chlorides and other substances became a national policy issue, the Ministry of Health and Welfare published *the Guidelines for Measures to Reduce Dioxin Emissions from Crematoria* (火葬場から排出されるダイオキシン類削減対策指針), which prompted crematoria nationwide to improve their facilities to reduce dioxin emissions.

In response to environmental issues, the *Crematorium Construction and Maintenance Manual* (火葬場の建設・維持管理マニュア

ル) was published in 2002 by the Japan Society of Environmental Crematory and has since been revised several times.[9] This manual includes operationalising the Air Pollution Control Act (1968), which regulates the emissions of soot, volatile organic compounds, and dust. Crematoria are not explicitly named in this act, but voluntary standards are determined by referring to those for waste incinerators. Recent proposals for revisions to the manual also highlight the need for greater regulation concerning environmental harms to cremation workers and provisions for burial/cremation during natural disasters.[10]

Notes

1 Seikatu Eisei Hōki Kenkyūkai 生活衛生法規研究会, ed., 逐条解説 墓地、埋葬等に関する法律 第3版 (東京: 第一法規, 2007), 103.

2 東京都, "墓地等の構造設備及び管理の基準等に関する条例", accessed February 22, 2024, www.reiki.metro.tokyo.lg.jp/reiki/reiki_hon bun/g101RG00000893.html.

3 Mori Kenji 森謙二, "人間（死者）の尊厳性と「埋葬義務」," 2010, in いま、この日本の家族, Iwakami Mami 岩上真珠, Suzuki Iwayumi 鈴木岩弓, Mori Kenji 森謙二, and Watanabe Hideki 渡辺秀樹 (東京: 弘文堂, 2010), 132–175.

4 NHK shuzaihan NHK取材班, さまよう遺骨 (東京：NHK出版, 2019).

5 Yagisawa Sōichi 八木澤壯一, "火葬場研究の目的と施設の概要: 火葬場の建築計画に関する研究I," 日本建築学会論文情報集 295 (September 1980), 96.

6 Ibid, 93.

7 Article 9 of the "Chiba City Ordinance on Permission to Operate Cemeteries, etc.". Research Institute for the Local Government, 千葉市墓地等の経営の許可等に関する条例, Accessed March 4, 2024, www1.g-reiki.net/chiba/reiki_honbun/g002RG00000785.html#e000000454.

8 Japan Society of Environmental Crematory 日本環境斎苑協会, 火葬場の建設・維持管理マニュアル (東京: 日本環境斎苑協会, 2002).

9 *Ibid.*

10 MHLW, 火葬場の設置管理運営基準の見直しに関する研究, 2016. Accessed March 2, 2024, https://mhlw-grants.niph.go.jp/system/files/2015/154061/201525014A_upload/201525014A0003.pdf

4 Demographic and Legal Frameworks

4.1 Mortality Statistics

Current demographic data on deaths in Japan can be obtained from the Ministry of Health, Labour and Welfare (MHLW) "Various Statistical Surveys" webpage,[1] or from e-Stat, the online portal for Japanese Government Statistics.[2] As described in Chapter 2, advances in medical technology, improved living standards, and the introduction of health insurance after WWII led to a significant decline in both the number and rate of death. In 1966, Japan recorded the lowest number of deaths per annum, 670,000, and in 1979 the lowest rate of death, 6%, since record keeping began.[3] Since then, both the number of deaths and the mortality rate have been on a gradual incline as the population ages, with the number of deaths hovering around 1.3 million per annum since 2016 (Figure 4.1). However, due to the impact of Covid-19, the number of deaths in 2022 increased significantly from 1.37 million in 2020 to 1.57 million in 2022[4]. However, as of May 2023, the cumulative number of deaths from Covid-19 alone was under 75,000.[5] This discrepancy is likely the result of people dying from other conditions related to Covid-19, including secondary infections, as well as delays in seeking medical care.

In 2022, the leading cause of death was malignant neoplasms or cancer (24.6%), followed by heart disease (excluding hypertension) (14.8%), and then senility (11.4%). These conditions alone account for nearly 50% of all deaths (Table 4.1). Malignant neoplasms have consistently been the leading cause of death since 1981. The proportion of senility has also continued to rise since 2001, which indicates that these deaths are predominantly distributed among the elderly. In fact, the number of deaths among people aged 75 years and over has

DOI: 10.4324/9781003451914-4

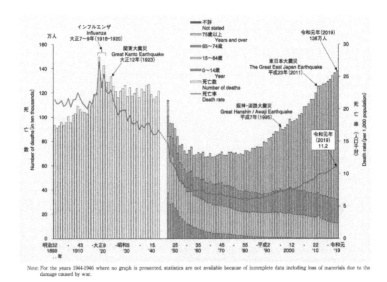

Note: For the years 1944-1946 where no graph is presented, statistics are not available because of incomplete data including loss of materials due to the damage caused by war.

Figure 4.1 Chart showing changes in the number of deaths and death rate in Japan over time. Based on data from the Ministry of Health, Labour and Welfare.

consistently exceeded 70% of all deaths in Japan in the last decade[6]. These demographic trends have a significant impact on the size and style of funerals (Chapter 7).

Data on disposal is also key to understanding Japanese death and funeral practice.[7] The two legal ways of disposing of human remains in Japan are cremation and burial. Statistics for each can be found in the annual Report on Public Health Administration and Services by the MHLW, which shows that in the 2021 financial year (April 2021–March 2022), the number of cremations was 1,512,973, and the number of burials was 462, for a total number of 1,512,973 body disposal cases. By percentage, this makes Japan's contemporary burial rate only 0.03% and the cremation rate 99.97%, indicating that almost all of the Japanese dead are cremated. Until very recently, cremation has been routinely accompanied by the interment of cremated remains in household graves. Burial was once the predominant disposal method in Japan. Until only 100 years ago, the rate of burial exceeded that of cremation (Figure 4.2) and in many areas the rate of burial has

Table 4.1 Leading causes of death in Japan (1947–2020)

	1st	2nd	3rd	4th	5th
1947	Tuberculosis	Pneumonia	Gastroenteritis	Cerebrovascular diseases	Senility
1950	Tuberculosis	Cerebrovascular diseases	Pneumonia	Gastroenteritis	Malignant neoplasms
1960	Cerebrovascular diseases	Malignant neoplasms	Heart diseases	Senility	Pneumonia
1970	Cerebrovascular diseases	Malignant neoplasms	Heart diseases	Accidents	Senility
1980	Cerebrovascular diseases	Malignant neoplasms	Heart diseases	Pneumonia	Senility
1990	Malignant neoplasms	Heart diseases	Cerebrovascular diseases	Pneumonia	Accidents
2000	Malignant neoplasms	Heart diseases	Cerebrovascular diseases	Pneumonia	Accidents
2010	Malignant neoplasms	Heart diseases	Cerebrovascular diseases	Pneumonia	Senility
2020	Malignant neoplasms	Heart diseases	Senility	Cerebrovascular diseases	Pneumonia

Note: Based on data from the Ministry of Health, Labour and Welfare.

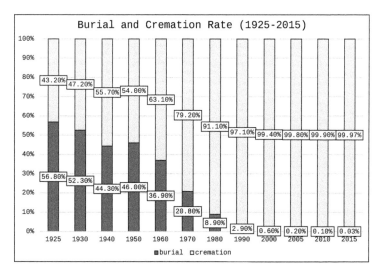

Figure 4.2 Chart showing changes in burial and cremation rates in Japan between 1925 and 2015. Reproduced with permission from the Ministry of Health, Labour and Welfare.

remained relatively high until recent decades. For example, in Iwate, Fukushima, Ibaraki, Tochigi, Yamanashi, Mie, Shiga and Nagasaki prefectures, around 3 to 8% of the deceased were buried until the late 1990s.[8] Currently, Kanagawa Prefecture (located south of Tokyo and encompassing Yokohama city) has the highest net number of burials in Japan (331 in the 2021 financial year), of which 322 were neonatal remains.

As cremation is now the expected practice for body disposal, many people in Japan appear to be uncomfortable with whole body burial. There have been many cases in which Muslim immigrants to Japan have been unable to acquire burial plots due to opposition from local residents (see section 10.5).[9] In Miyagi Prefecture, which experienced a mass death event of nearly 40% of the average annual death toll after the 2011 Great East Japan earthquake and tsunami, the number of bodies overwhelmed deathcare service providers. As an emergency measure, beginning in March 2011, some local authorities decided to temporarily bury the bodies of over 2,000 victims. However, after vocal objections from bereaved families and the community, the bodies began to be exhumed in April 2011, just one month after burial. By November of that same year, all the bodies had been exhumed and cremated.[10]

4.2 Legal Frameworks

4.2.1 Death Registration

In the event of a death, Article 86(1) of the Family Register Act (1947) stipulates that the person obliged to notify government services of the death must do so within seven days from the date on which they came to know of the death.[11] The persons obliged to submit a notice of death are, in descending order, cohabiting relatives of the deceased, cohabiting other persons, owners of the residence, and landlords or administrators of the residence or land (Article 87, [1] and [2]). The notification of death is submitted with a Death Certificate (死亡診断書 *shibō shindansho*) or Certificate of Postmortem Examination (死体検案書 *shitai ken'ansho*), except in exceptional circumstances. The standard form consists of a two-page spread, with the Notification of Death on the left and the Death Certificate (or Certificate of Postmortem Examination) on the right (Figure 4.3). Deaths are reported to the prefectural authority where the person died (Article 88, [1]).

The determination of death is the exclusive prerogative of medical doctors, and Death Certificates or Certificates of Postmortem Examination can only be issued by them (Medical Practitioners' Act, Article 19, [2]).[12] The Death Certificate or Certificate of Postmortem Examination has an important role, as it provides medical and legal proof of death and serves as the basis for compiling cause-of-death statistics.[13] Funeral Directors can only handle a body after legal death has been confirmed by a doctor.

Generally, a doctor completes the Death Certificate when their patient is found to have died from a known disease or condition for which they were examined before death. In all other cases, a Certificate of Postmortem Examination is prepared. A Death Certificate cannot be completed in the case of a deceased who was not seen by a doctor before death, for example, in the case of a sudden death or if the patient was not seen by a doctor for an extended period. In these later cases, a Certificate of Postmortem Examination is completed (Article 20). When a doctor is not present at the time of death, a Death Certificate

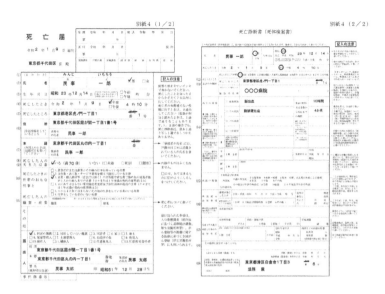

Figure 4.3 A sample of the Notification of Death form (left) and Death Certification or Certificate of Postmortem Examination form (right). Reproduced with permission from the Ministry of Justice.

can still be issued, if the doctor examined the deceased in the period leading up to their death and then can examine the body postmortem to establish that the death was related to the treating condition. If a Death Certificate cannot be issued, a Certificate of Postmortem Examination is issued following the autopsy and is completed by a coroner, or a doctor commissioned by the police. The autopsy is to investigate the possibility that the death was the result of something other than natural causes. Even if the death was likely due to illness or natural causes, if the cause of death is unclear to a doctor who has not examined the patient before death, then an autopsy is ordered.[14] The doctor must notify the local police station within 24 hours if any abnormality is detected in the corpse (Article 22). In that case, a Death Certificate or a Certificate of Post Mortem Examination is issued, including the results of the autopsy and other findings by the investigating authority.

The municipal authority that receives the notification of death issues a permit for cremation or burial. The law states that in reflection of the people's religious sentiments, public health, and welfare, it is prohibited and punishable to bury or cremate a corpse without receiving this permission (Graveyard and Burial Act, Articles 4 and 21 [1]). If the cremated remains are to be buried in a cemetery after cremation (as they usually are), this permit must be certified by the crematorium and submitted to the cemetery administrator (Chapter 10).

The regulations for notification of stillbirths, defined as the death of a foetus after the fourth month of pregnancy, has separate rules from those adult deaths that fall under the Family Register Act (1947). The Code on Notification of Stillbirths (1946) states that all stillbirths must be reported within seven days of the delivery. This report must be accompanied by a Certificate of Stillbirth or a Certificate of Stillbirth Examination, which is to be completed by a doctor or midwife (Article 4). The notification must be submitted to the local authorities where the notifier is located or where the stillbirth occurred (Article 4). The person notifying of the stillbirth should be the father, or if the father is unable to do so for unavoidable reasons, the mother, and if both parents are unable to do so for unavoidable reasons, a cohabitant, the doctor or midwife who attended the stillbirth, or other witnesses, or non-relatives, in that order (Article 7).

4.2.2 Disposal of the Dead

The disposal of human remains in Japan is largely governed by the Graveyard and Burial Act or "GBA", which was first enacted in 1948. The main purpose of this law is to ensure that the disposal of human remains and the management of cemeteries, crematoria, and columbaria "conform to the religious sentiments of the people and are carried out without hindrance from the standpoint of public health and other public welfare" (Article 1). This chapter focuses on the disposal of bodies, while Chapter 9 describes aspects of the GBA relevant to crematoria, and Chapter 10 describes aspects of the GBA relevant to cemeteries.

In Japan, burial or cremation may only take place at least 24 hours after a death or stillbirth, "except as otherwise provided by other legislation" (Article 3). This is to ensure that there is no possibility of resuscitation of the deceased, a provision carried over from the Cemeteries and Burial Control Regulations of 1884. However, this does not apply in the case of a foetus that cannot be resuscitated or in the case of a stillbirth of less than seven months' gestation (Proviso to Article 3).

In this provision of the GBA, the phrase "except as otherwise provided by other legislation" refers to Article 30 of the Act on the Prevention of Infectious Diseases and Medical Care for Patients with Infectious Diseases (1998).[15] This Act restricts or prohibits the movement of a corpse and allows cremation within 24 hours if the deceased is suspected of having contracted a designated infectious disease, such as class I, II, and III infectious diseases, or a new type of influenza. The act further stipulates that bodies suspected of having contracted designated infectious diseases must be cremated, except when authorized by the prefectural governor. Article 15 of the Mariners' Act specifies that bodies may be disposed of via sea burial in the event of the death of a person who was onboard the ship while it was underway.

Covid-19, which spread through Japan beginning in early 2020, was initially classified as a "a new influenza and other infectious disease" (class II equivalent) but was downgraded to a class V infectious disease on the 8th of May 2023. This means that those deceased from Covid-19 were previously allowed to be cremated within a period of 24 hours after death, but this is no longer permitted.[16]

Although cremation is now standard, whole body burial is not prohibited, and the GBA clearly states that burial is legal. However, some local authorities have prohibited burial within their region.[17] As almost all deceased are currently cremated, burial/cremation permits are often described simply as cremation permits in Japan today.[18] While whole body burial is not impossible in Japan, significant preparations are required for those wishing to undertake this practice. This includes clearly indicating one's desire to be buried before death, securing cemetery space, and finding a funeral company that will facilitate the practice.

In the case of cremation, the incineration of the body itself can be carried out without significant administrative difficulty, but the subsequent handling of the cremated remains has been the subject of much debate in recent years. The system of body disposal outlined in the GBA is based on the interment of remains in a cemetery or columbarium. However, in recent years, new methods of handling cremated remains that go beyond the framework of the GBA have emerged. Examples include pulverising remains to ash (cremulation),[19] scattering them at sea or in nature, and keeping remains at home for an extended period of time.

In the first place, as stipulated in Article 4 (1) of the GBA, the interment of remains outside of a place authorised as a cemetery is strictly prohibited, and violations may result in charges related to the abandonment of a corpse under Article 190 of the Penal Code (1907). Accordingly, the scattering of ashes outside cemeteries had long been considered illegal. However, the situation changed drastically in 1991 when a private organisation promoting ash scattering began implementing this practice at sea.[20] The Ministry of Justice's opinion, issued this year, and a report published in 1998 by the Environmental Health Bureau of the MHLW stated that scattering ashes was not a problem unless it caused public health problems or injured public religious sentiment.[21] Scattering has subsequently and gradually become more popular. However, as ash scattering is not covered by existing laws, unregulated scattering did cause problems in its early stages, and some municipalities have banned it by ordinance. In response, in 2014, the Japan Marine Ash Scattering General Incorporated Association, which was established in 2012 by businesses involved in ocean scattering, published best practice guidelines, and worked to promote scattering practices that do not offend existing laws.[22] Although no national laws or regulations on ash scattering have yet been created, the MHLW published guidelines for scattering providers in 2021, and this has contributed to the practice achieving a certain level of standardisation across Japan.[23]

Additionally, the practice of retaining some or all of the cremated remains at home, known as *temoto kuyō* (手元供養), has become widespread since the 2000s (Chapter 11). This does not constitute 'interment' in the sense ascribed by the GBA. While there have been no significant legal objections to this practice, some people still regard it as technically illegal or distasteful.[24]

4.2.3 Unclaimed Dead

In Japan, since the early modern period (c.17th–19th century), next of kin have been obligated to dispose of the dead and perform rituals. Since the late 19th century, laws have been put into place by government to handle the unclaimed dead, predominantly those who fall ill and die during travel from their domicile (行旅死亡人 *kōryo sibōnin*).[25]

Three legal frameworks govern the disposal of the unclaimed or unknown dead: the GBA, the Act on Treatment of Persons Who Contracted Disease or Died on Journey (ATPCDDJ) (1899), and the Public Assistance Act (1950). Article 9 of the GBA stipulates that the prefectural authority where a death occurred is responsible for the burial or cremation of that body if no one related to the deceased is identifiable or contactable. This article does not apply to those whose names and addresses are unknown, who are covered instead by the ATPCDDJ. Article 7 of the ATPCDDJ also places responsibility with the relevant municipal authority.[26] In the case of welfare recipients who are bereaved and unable to pay for a funeral and cremation because of lack of funds, or where the welfare recipient themselves died without relatives, a third party, such as the landlord or a welfare commissioner, is responsible for conducting the funeral and body disposal. The national government provides funeral assistance expenses to the person conducting the funeral, according to Article 18 of the Public Assistance Act (Chapter 8). However, the maximum funeral assistance payment is approximately ¥200,000 per adult, and this amount only covers encoffining and cremation, leaving no funds for a funeral ceremony.

Most people who die in Japan today are elderly, and with the declining birth rate, may elderly live alone without close relatives nearby. Even when the deceased's identity and living relatives are known, such relatives may refuse to take responsibility for the body disposal and funeral, citing grounds of estrangement. In such cases, the local authority is ultimately held responsible in accordance with Article 9 of the GBA. This has placed an ever-increasing financial burden on municipal governments.[27] In the 2022 financial year, the number of public funeral assistance payments was the highest to date, with 52,000 cases costing ¥11 billion.[28]

Notes

1 Ministry of Health, Labour and Welfare (MHLW) 厚生労働省, 各種統計調査, accessed July 24, 2023, www.mhlw.go.jp/toukei_hakusho/toukei/.
2 "e-Stat, The Portal Site of Official Statistics of Japan," accessed July 24, 2023, www.e-stat.go.jp/.
3 Director-General for Statistics and Information Policy, *Vital Statistics in Japan 2019* (Tokyo: MHLW, 2018), 27.
4 MHLW 厚生労働省, 令和4年(2022)人口動態統計月報年計(概数)の概況, accessed July 24, 2023, www.mhlw.go.jp/toukei/saikin/hw/jinkou/geppo/nengai22/index.html.
5 NHK, 国内の感染者数・死者数, accessed July 24, 2023, www3.nhk.or.jp/news/special/coronavirus/data-all/.
6 MHLW 厚生労働省, 人口動態統計月報年計.

7 As per the industry standard in English, we use the term 'disposal' here to refer to the handling of human remains, despite its negative connotations.

8 MHLW, "Report on Public Health Administration and Services FY1997", accessed December 20, 2023, www.mhlw.go.jp/english/database/db-hss/rophas.html

9 Suzuki Kantarō 鈴木貫太郎, ルポ 日本の土葬 (東京: 宗教問題, 2023).

10 Suzuki Iwayumi 鈴木岩弓, "東日本大震災時の土葬選択にみる死者観念," in 今を生きる：東日本大震災から明日へ！復興と再生への提言1人間として, eds. Zakota Yutaka 座小田豊 and Ozaki Akihiro 尾崎彰宏 (東京: 東北大学出版会, 2012), 103–21.

11 If the death occurs outside Japan, the notification must be made within three months.

12 Mori Shigeru 森茂, 日本の葬送・墓地 (京都: 法律文化社, 2013), 84.

13 MHLW, *Manual to fill in a death certificate*, 2023, www.mhlw.go.jp/toukei/manual/dl/manual_r04.pdf

14 Himonya Hajime 碑文谷創, 葬儀概論 四訂版 (東京: 葬祭ディレクター技能審査協会, 2017), 88.

15 Seikatu Eisei Hōki Kenkyūkai 生活衛生法規研究会, ed., 逐条解説 墓地、埋葬等に関す法律 (東京: 第一法規, 2007), 17–9.

16 MHLW and METI, 新型コロナウイルスにより亡くなられた方及びその疑いがある方の処置、搬送、葬儀、火葬等に関するガイドライン, accessed June 14, 2023, www.mhlw.go.jp/content/001107743.pdf, 23.

17 For example, all 23 wards in Tokyo prohibit burial. Kasōkenkyukyōkai Ricchibukai火葬研究会立地部会 ed., 火葬場の立地 (東京: 日本経済評論社, 2004), 97.

18 Himonya 碑文谷, 葬儀概論 四訂版, 101.

19 The practice of cremation in Japan preserves whole bone fragments, and cremulation is rarely practiced (Chapter 9).

20 Mark Rowe, "Grave Changes: Scattering Ashes in Contemporary Japan," *Japanese Journal of Religious Studies* 30, no. 1–2 (2003): 85–118.

21 Murata Masumi 村田ますみ and Takeuchi Yūkō 武内優宏, "日本における海洋散骨30年のあゆみ," 葬送文化 24 (2023): 85–109.

22 Japan Marine Ash Scattering General Incorporated Association 日本海洋散骨協会, accessed July 26, 2023, https://kaiyousou.or.jp/guideline.html.

23 MHLW 厚生労働省, 散骨に関するガイドライン（事業者向け）, accessed July 26, 2023, www.mhlw.go.jp/stf/seisakunitsuite/bunya/0000123872.html.

24 Seikatu Eisei Hōki Kenkyūkai 生活衛生法規研究会, 逐条解説 墓地、埋葬等に関する法律, 19.

25 Yamada Shinya 山田慎也, "引き取り手のない故人の葬送と助葬制度," in 無縁社会の葬送と墓, eds. Yamada Shinya and 山田慎也 and Doi Hiroshi 土居浩 (東京: 吉川弘文館, 2022), 37–58.

26 Seikatu Eisei Hōki Kenkyūkai 生活衛生法規研究会, 40.

27 Kotani Midori 小谷みどり, "火葬場が足りない？「数日待ち」のからくりとは……," 朝日新聞デジタル, May 15, 2019, www.asahi.com/relife/article/12355405.

28 Asahi Shinbun Digital朝日新聞デジタル, 公費で葬祭費負担、過去最多, October 23, 2023, www.asahi.com/articles/DA3S15773460.html?fbclid=IwAR0RVGOmqls1z229E_VQ4BbdsdPUWoW5EQa8HvUBjf5YVf0eywHMuWnOsbI.

5 Religion

Japan is home to multiple religious traditions. According to a survey by the Ministry of Education, Culture, Sports, Science and Technology (MEXT), 70% of the Japanese population is Shinto (88,959,345 persons), 66.7% is Buddhist (84,835,110 persons), 1.5% is Christian (1,909,757 persons), and 5.8% hold 'other beliefs' (7,403,560 persons).[1] This category of 'other beliefs' includes various world religions and new religious movements. The combined percentages well exceed the total population of Japan, indicating significant religious pluralism or syncretism, particularly between Buddhist and Shinto populations.

At the same time, other representative surveys of the Japanese population indicate that only 36% of people describe themselves as religious, with the vast majority categorising themselves as non-religious.[2] Japanese people commonly refer to themselves as non-religious (無宗教 *mushūkyō*), while occasionally praying at Shinto shrines for good luck in an upcoming exam or business venture, attending Christian-style wedding ceremonies, and hiring Buddhist priests to conduct funeral rites. This apparent contradiction can be understood with reference to the history of the term religion (宗教 *shūkyō*) in Japan, which is a relatively recent coinage, emerging in the 19th century, and largely used to describe institutional religious traditions not folk practices.[3] As such, Japanese people are primed to view some activities, like attending Shinto festivals or visiting Buddhist graves, as more of a cultural practice than a religious one. Simultaneously, there is evidence that non-religiosity is on the rise in Japan. In a 2018 survey, only 26% of respondents answered that they had strong, significant, or some religious faith (信仰心あり *shinkōshin ari*), outside of the context of rites of passage (e.g. funerals, coming of

DOI: 10.4324/9781003451914-5

age days, weddings, etc.) (compared to 32% when the survey was first conducted in 1998).[4] In the same survey, 48% of respondents reported that they prayed to 'gods or buddhas' (神仏 *shinbutsu*) more than once or twice a year.

As a rite of passage (冠婚葬祭 *kankon sōsai*), funerals in Japan are dominated by Buddhism, even amongst the 'non-religious', with additional historical influences from Shintoism (described in Section 5.2), Confucianism, and folk practices. Confucianism is a system of thought originating in China that emphasises personal ethics, including filial piety, and was transmitted to Japan alongside Buddhism, from around the 6th century. Transcending any particular religious tradition, ancestor veneration (先祖供養 *senzo kuyō*) is a popular cultural practice that incorporates teachings and artefacts of many different traditions. It describes a belief that the deceased gradually transition from individual spirits of the dead to household ancestors. These ancestors 'look over' or provide guidance to the living members of the household in the form of good fortune, financial windfalls, and fertility. In turn, the living must care for the dead through acts of service and making offerings.[5] These offerings are carried out at the household grave and at the domestic Buddhist altar. If abandoned or neglected, the dead may transform into bondless buddhas (無縁仏 *muenbotoke*) or hungry ghosts (餓鬼 *gaki*), who haunt the living and may cause harm by way of natural disasters or illness. These abandoned dead may also be created by 'bad deaths', such as through suicide, murder, wars, natural disasters, or death without descendants.

The following sections explain death and funeral practice within Japan's major religions.

5.1 Buddhism

5.1.1 Context

Buddhism is a world religion with diverse branches, teachings, rituals, and cultural expressions. It is founded on the teachings of Siddhartha Gautama, a sage and wandering ascetic who lived during the 6th or 5th century BCE in South Asia. In Buddhist cosmology, all beings of the universe are born into and move through cycles of death and rebirth, known as *samsara* (Sk.) or *rinne* (Jp.). The Buddha taught that this cycle is fuelled by karma, or the cause and effect of actions.

Put simply, intentionally good acts give rise to good effects, and intentionally bad acts give rise to bad effects. Buddhism sets forth a code of wisdom, practice, and ethics aimed at reducing suffering by cultivating good karma. For most beings, cycles of samsara are unending. But some beings may become enlightened and escape the cycle, as the historical Buddha did. All schools of Buddhism see death as a particularly important spiritual transition and an opportunity for moving toward enlightenment.

Buddhism has been practised in Japan since at least the 6th century CE. As noted in Chapter 2, it was quickly adopted by the ruling classes and Emperor, with scholars and monks regularly sent to China and Korea to bring back new knowledge. Japanese Buddhism today consists of many different schools, originating overseas or born of domestic reform movements, particularly in the Kamakura period (1185–1333). Most Japanese Buddhism is classified as Mahāyāna or 'Great Vehicle' Buddhism, one of two major branches of Buddhism worldwide (alongside Theravāda). Consistent with this lineage, schools of Japanese Buddhism tend to emphasise an individual's spiritual path toward becoming a bodhisattva (菩薩 *bosatsu*), a compassionate spiritual being dedicated to securing the enlightenment of others. Japanese Buddhism is also characterised by a number of distinct teachings, including the concept of emptiness and the existence of a Buddha-nature.

During the Heian period (794–1185) death became entrusted to Buddhism[6] following the adoption of monastic funeral rites by the elite Heian court nobility, and eventually, common people. Then, under the rule of the Tokugawa Shogunate (1603–1867), the 'temple-parishioner system' made it compulsory for all households to register with a Buddhist temple and directed temples to conduct funeral rites. The system was officially abolished in the Meiji period, but the association between temples and households remains strong. Indeed, temples derive significant financial support from providing these services and from the management of graves. Utilising a descriptive term first coined by Tamamuro Taijō in a neutral sense, several commentators thus negatively describe Japanese Buddhism as "funeral Buddhism" (葬式仏教 *sōshiki bukkyō*) for its (almost exclusive) focus on death.[7]

According to 2022 figures from MEXT there are approximately 83,988 Buddhist organisations and 353,635 Buddhist teachers operating in contemporary Japan[8]. Over 100 Buddhist organisations belong to the Japan Buddhist Federation (JBF). The vast majority of priests do not live ascetic lifestyles upholding monastic precepts (*vinaya*). Indeed, priests are usually not celibate, often marry, and temples are regularly passed down as family businesses. Some schools of Japanese Buddhism have been intentionally non-renunciatory and non-celibate since their founding, for example, *Jōdo Shinshū* or 'True Pure Land' Buddhism (founded 13th century). More broadly, this custom spread in the 19th century in the context of the national government's persecution of radical Buddhist schools.[9] Unlike in many other Buddhist countries, it is also unusual for lay Japanese Buddhists to ever take monastic precepts during their life time. However, most Japanese people go through 'posthumous ordination' as part of Buddhist funeral rites, which were historically performed for monastics (Chapter 6).

There are multiple schools of Buddhism operating within Japan today. Each have different key texts, teachings, and organisational structures. Some emphasise activities like chanting mantras or copying sutras, while other traditions focus on activities like meditation and pilgrimage. Most lay practitioners encounter Buddhism when attending funeral and memorial services or as part of tourism at famous temples. Many homes have a domestic Buddhist altar (仏壇 *butsudan*), which enshrines an icon of a Buddha, mortuary tablets, and other ritual goods (see Section 11.2.3).

Pure Land Buddhism is the school with the largest number of followers today. Pure Land Buddhism is focused on achieving rebirth in the "western Pure Land of Utmost Bliss" (極楽浄土 *gokuraku jōdo*) and the veneration of Amida Buddha (the Buddha of Infinite Light). While some schools of Japanese Buddhism emphasise the ability of practitioners to reach enlightenment through their own power (自力 *jiriki*), Pure Land Buddhism suggests that outside help (他力 *tariki*) is required, specifically, the power of Amida Buddha. This is achieved through recitation of the *nenbutsu* mantra and deathbed visualisation and contemplation.[10]

5.1.2 Funeral Practice

Most contemporary Japanese funerals are Buddhist. According to one 2020s survey,[11] 89.4% of funerals were conducted with the involvement of a Buddhist priest. Buddhist funeral rites are focused on consoling the spirits of the dead to assist them in their journey through intermediary states between life, death, and finally rebirth, either in this world, or in some superior realm closer to Buddhahood (成仏 *jōbutsu*). The format of Japanese Buddhist funerals was conceived of in the mediaeval period within the Zen school, where it originated as a funeral rite for deceased priests, the *motsugo sasō* (没後作僧), before being spread amongst the broader populace (see Section 2.2). This progression of this service is described in Chapter 7. Broadly, it includes the rituals of the wake, funeral, and cremation, followed by years of memorial rites.

The sutras read at funerals and memorials differ between Buddhist schools, however the central component facilitates the deceased's acceptance of the Buddhist precepts or moral code (受戒 *jukai*) and their subsequent induction (引導 *indō*) into a posthumous priesthood.[12] One prominent exception to this format is funerals conducted within Pure Land Buddhism, which teaches that all beings can attain buddhahood in the Pure Land by embracing the power of Amida Buddha. In this tradition, the language of 'farewell' is not used in regard to the funeral and the priest does not make prayers for the welfare of the deceased's spirit (as it is already guaranteed). For the same reason, there is no tradition of dressing the deceased in special mortuary clothes (死装束 *shinishōzoku*) (see Chapter 7).

In most Japanese Buddhist schools, it is common for individuals to receive a precept name or *kaimyō* (戒名) upon death. The True Pure Land school calls this name *hōmyō* (法名), as their followers do not take posthumous precepts, and Nichiren school calls it *hōgō* (法号).[13] This name is used during the funeral service and engraved on the mortuary tablet and gravestone. *Kaimyō* are purchased for a significant cost from temples, leading to critiques of Japanese Buddhism as profiteering from death (see Section 8.1.3).[14]

Buddhism also influences the boundaries of who or what is subject to funerary rites in Japan. In Buddhist cosmology, humans are not uniquely endowed with a spirit or soul. The teaching of dependent origination (Sk. Pratītyasamutpāda, Jp. *engi*) states that all phenomena are interdependent and arise in relation to one another. Buddhist temples have long histories of holding memorial services for non-humans, including animals and pets (e.g. whales, monkeys, and dogs), tools (e.g. scissors, knives, and sewing needles), and machines (e.g. computers and robots). Rituals are also held for *mizuko* (水子), a category that includes aborted, stillborn, and miscarried foetuses (see Section 11.1 on *kuyō*).

5.2 Shintoism and Folk Practices

5.2.1 Context

Shintoism is a religion based on the diverse set of folk rituals and beliefs of the ethnic Japanese people which predate (and continue after) the arrival of Buddhism, Confucianism, and other world religions. It is highly regional and usually discussed as distinct from the religious practices of Indigenous populations, such as the Ainu or Ryukyuan peoples.

Shintoism is diverse and decentralised, with no central authority, founder, set of teachings or ethics, or canonical text. Instead, Shintoism draws heavily on local custom. It has been described as polytheistic and animist, revolving around the veneration of supernatural beings known as *kami* (神). *Kami* are manifold in number and exist in all manner of phenomena, including forces of nature (e.g. thunder), prominent natural features (e.g. mountains), notable people, and ancestors. The practice of Shintoism involves living in harmony with *kami*, through cultivating their good fortune and blessings while pacifying or appeasing wrathful or dangerous *kami*.

The distinction between 'folk religious practice' and 'Shintoism' is debated, as is the latter's status as a world religion of a similar type, for example, to Christianity or Islam. When Buddhism first entered Japan, rampant syncretisation (神仏習合 *shinbutsu shūgō*) made the two functionally indistinguishable in many cases. A major event in the development of Shinto as a religion was the nationalist movement of the Meiji era (1868–1912), which enforced the separation of Buddhism and Shinto, and founded 'State Shinto' as a distinct entity, with the Emperor positioned as a *kami*. This system was formally abolished in the context of Japan's defeat in WWII by the Shinto Directive, issued by the Supreme Commander for the Allied Forces in December 1945. Today, the Association of Shinto Shrines or *Jinja Honchō* (神社本庁), founded in 1946, is the chief administrative organisation for Shintoism. It oversees over 80,000 shrines, united under the teachings of the Ise Grand Shrine, through regulation of ritual performance, the training of priests, and education of followers.

Across Japan, there are innumerable shrines devoted to different *kami*. Larger shrines may be staffed by priests, known as *kannushi*, and assisted by *miko* (shrine maidens). People interact with Shintoism by visiting shrines to pray for good luck in business, school, or family life; by purchasing protective amulets; and drawing fortunes. Shrines host important rites of passage, such as weddings and coming of age ceremonies, as well as large public festivals or *matsuri*. Festivals often revolve around the ritualised transport of shrines through the streets and/or making timely offerings to a particular *kami* in line with the agricultural calendar. Alongside large public shrines, there are also innumerable unaffiliated micro-shrines that are tended to by the local community. Further, per a survey conducted in 2006, 43.8% of homes have a Shinto shrine (神棚 *kamidana*),[15] at which rice, sake, and other fresh produce may be offered to pray for the prosperity of the household.

Achieving and maintaining a state of purity and vitality is a major focus of Shintoism. This can be seen in the practices of ritualised washing or bathing, for example, cleansing one's hands and mouth with water at the entrance to a shrine. Three major spiritual forces are important to understanding this worldview: *hare*, which refers to that which is vital, extraordinary, or sacred; *ke*, which refers to ordinary life and growth, and finally *kegare*, which refers to pollution or impurity.[16] Death, bodily fluids, natural disaster, crime, and illness generate *kegare* or pollution, which drains the body of its regular energies or *ke*. This condition can be countered by revitalising one's stores of sacred energy (*hare*), through positive and enlivening rituals or festivals.

As the impurity of death is contagious, it is important for those who come into contact with it to perform ritual purification rites (*harai* or *misogi*). These usually involve natural forces like water, fire, or mineral salt.[17] A minority of Japanese households are affiliated with Shinto shrines (rather than Buddhist temples) and perform Shinto funerals, but such purification customs influence Japanese death culture more broadly. For example, at many funerals or wakes, purifying salt is distributed to attendees as a means to protect them from the contamination of death spreading into everyday life. However, these traditions do not occur at all funerals, such as those held with Pure Land Buddhist or Christian rites.

5.2.2 Funeral Practice

A very small percentage of Japanese funerals are conducted with Shinto rites, known as *shinsōsai* (神葬祭). In the 2020s, Shinto funerals made up just 3.9% of all funeral rites.[18] These rites are a modern production, being only held publicly since the Meiji period (1868–1912) in the context of the weakening of the Buddhist temple-parishioner system. Broadly, Shinto funerals are focused on transforming the dead into guardian ancestors of the family and on returning the household to a state of normalcy after the misfortune of death.[19]

It is customary for a death to be first reported (帰幽奉告 *kiyū hōkoku*) to the deity of the household Shinto shrine (祖霊舎 *sōreisha*). The doors of the shrine are then closed and a white piece of paper (神棚封じ *kamidana-fūji*) is wrapped around the shrine in order to protect it from being contaminated by the impurity of death. This paper remains through to the conclusion of the funeral. In some cases, a protective sword (守り刀 *mamorikatana*) may also be placed beside the deceased so as to ward them against evil spirits.

The deceased is laid out with their head facing north, dressed in white kimono, and covered with a white cloth. A folding screen is erected, and a small altar is set up next to the deceased, arranged with rice, salt, water, and other snacks or drinks that the deceased enjoyed. The deceased is then placed in a coffin.

The wake takes place at a ceremony hall or home. Given the threat of pollution, wakes and funerals are not usually held at Shinto shrines. A Shinto priest presides and recites ceremonial prayers (祭文 *saibun*). The event may also be accompanied by musicians playing *gagaku* or Japanese classic music. It is common for the bereaved family to give prayers and make offerings of branches of greenery. These offerings, known as *tamagushi* (玉串), are constructed from branches of the sakaki tree and decorated with strips of white paper.

The wake is followed by the *senreisai* (遷霊祭, or mitama utsushi), in which the spirit of the deceased is transferred from the corpse to a mortuary tablet, known as the reiji (霊爾). As the spirit is transferred, the musical composition *senreishi* is played and the lights of the facility are extinguished, to reproduce the darkness of night, when the spirit is said to be mobile. After this ceremony, the lights are turned on, and attendees gather before the mortuary tablet for final prayers.

The funeral ceremony generally takes place the next day. It begins with attendees ceremonially washing their hands. The presiding priest then ritually purifies the attendees by the sung recitation of prayers. The ceremony proceeds with recitations of prayers, instrumental music, readings of condolences and offerings of *tamagushi* branches by the assembled guests.

A procession of mourners, carrying the coffin, flowers, food offerings, portraits of the deceased, and flags with the name of the deceased, transport the coffin to the crematorium, or rarely, burial site. It is customary for mourners to go immediately to the grave after the cremation for the interment of cremated remains. However, in recent years, many people have begun to store cremated remains for extended periods of time in the family home. The remains may then be interred at on a special occasion or anniversary, such as the 50th day or one year anniversary.

After the funeral, *kikasai* (帰家祭) or a 'homecoming ceremony' may take place, for the purposes of purifying the attendees. People wash their hands in salt and water and announce the end of the funeral at the domestic shrine. Feasts for attendees are also common.

5.3 Minority Religions

5.3.1 *Context*

Minority religions in Japan include those brought to Japan via migration and cultural exchange, such as Christianity and Islam, as well as 'New Religions' that have emerged within Japan, such as Sōka Gakkai and Tenrikyō. Major world religions are represented in small minorities in Japan. Christians are spread among denominations and are predominantly located in Western Japan, including Nagasaki and Kyūshū, where Portuguese missionaries first arrived in Japan in the mid-16th century. Japanese new religions (新宗教 *shinshūkyō*) describe a diverse number of spiritual organisations and movements founded since the mid-19th century. Many are deeply syncretic, often blending aspects of Buddhism, folk religious practice, Shinto, and Christianity.

Adherents to minority religions in Japan may face hurdles to accessing specialised, appropriate deathcare services, given the predominance of Buddhist organisations in delivering deathcare to the general populace. Most notably, whole body burial is difficult to access within contemporary Japan, with only a limited number of cemeteries across the country offering this service, often at a significant cost (see Chapter 10). Minority religions have also had a contentious relationship with the Japanese state and broader populace throughout history. Christianity was formally banned in 1612 under the Tokugawa Shogunate (the ban was lifted in 1873), and there are several historical examples of missionaries and converts being taxed, harassed, or killed. As such, many converts of this period concealed their faith and were known as "hidden Christians" (隠れキリシタン *kakure kirishitan*).

In the modern era, instances of religiously-motivated violence have also damaged the reputation of organised religion. Most notably, the deadly 1995 sarin gas attacks on Tokyo subways, carried out by members of the new religious movement Aum Shinrikyō, lead to significant negative public sentiment and increased government surveillance for new religious movements.

5.3.2 Funeral Practices

Summaries of the funeral services in Christian communities and in one new religious community, Sōka Gakkai, are given here as examples of minority religious practice in Japan.

5.3.2.1 Christianity

Christianity is a monotheistic religion, founded on the teachings of Jesus of Nazareth, who lived and died in the 1st century CE. It is the world's largest religion, with over 2.4 billion followers, and has several major branches, including Catholicism, Protestantism, Eastern Orthodoxy, and Oriental Orthodoxy. Christians believe in the promise of eternal life in heaven, where they will be reunited with God. For some, the fulfilment of this promise is guaranteed upon for the acceptance of Jesus as their saviour, for others it is also the result of good works. Alongside the number of Japanese converts, Christianity has a broader cultural presence in Japan through the modern wedding ceremony and organisations that provide hospice services.[20] However, only 1.4% population has a Christian funeral.[21]

Japanese Christian funerals are usually held at a church or funeral hall. Depending on the denomination of the deceased, the service may include readings from the Bible, a sermon, and songs. Catholic services may take the form of a funeral mass. Conventional Buddhist elements of the funeral service, such as the offering of incense, mortuary tablet, and prayer beads, are largely absent. Some elements may be substituted with equivalent rituals. For example, attendees may be asked to come forward to the front of the room and place flowers upon the coffin (as with the offering of greenery in Shinto funerals

Figure 5.1 Grave in the 'Eri Hidden Christian Graveyard' on Hisaka Island, Goto Islands, Nagasaki Prefecture, 27th August 2023. Reproduced with permission of photographer, Dr Gwyn McClelland.

or incense in Buddhist funerals).[22] Condolence payments given to the bereaved family are referred to as "flower fees" (御花料 *ohanaryō*) rather than "incense fees" (香典 *kōden*).[23] Similarly, Christian graves (Figure 5.1) often mimic the general style of Buddhist household graves, but with the addition of a cross.

5.3.2.2 *Sōka Gakkai*

Sōka Gakkai is a Japanese new religion founded in the 1930s and 1940s and based on the teachings of the 13th-century Buddhist priest, Nichiren. It focuses on the teachings of the Lotus Sutra and the merits of chanting the mantra of that sutra, *namu myōhō renge kyō*. Unlike conventional Japanese Buddhist organisations, Sōka Gakkai today is led by unordained laypeople and has no priesthood, following the organisation's break from mainstream Nichiren Buddhism in 1991.

Domestically, the organisation claims a membership of 8.27 million households and 2.8 million members outside of Japan.[24]

Sōka Gakkai values the doctrine of a buddha nature and teaches that the fundamental purpose of faith is to attain buddhahood. Unlike many other schools of Japanese Buddhism, the organisation suggests that people can manifest buddhahood through devoted practice in one's lifetime (一生成仏 *isshō jōbutsu*), before the moment of death. Still, death is an important occasion for friends and family to come together and pray for the happiness (冥福 *meifuku*) of the deceased.

Funerals conducted in Sōka Gakkai are referred to as 'friend funerals' or *yūjinsō*[25] and have a distinctive form. The standardised funeral service emerged in 1991 after the organisation left Nichiren Buddhism. As befitting a lay organisation, funerals are led by a representative of the bereaved (usually a close friend or relative), rather than priests. No posthumous name (*kaimyō*) or mortuary tablet (*ihai*) is created or used. Further, funeral attendees are not required to give condolence payments or presents. The organisation further discourages ongoing memorial services for the dead, including the 49-day ceremony or death anniversary services. However, annual memorial services are held at regional halls during the Buddhist festivals of Higan and Obon.

Notes

1 Agency for Cultural Affairs 文化庁, *宗教年鑑 令和2年版*, December 2020, www.bunka.go.jp/tokei_hakusho_shuppan/hakusho_nenjihokoku sho/shukyo_nenkan/pdf/r02nenkan.pdf.

2 Kobayashi Toshiyuki 小林利行, "日本人の宗教的意識や行動はど う変わったか," *NHK Broadcasting Research and Surveys*, April 2019, www.nhk.or.jp/bunken/research/yoron/20190401_7.html.

3 Ama Toshimaro 阿満利麿, *日本人はなぜ無宗教なのか* (東京: ちくま新書, 1996); Hans Martin Krämer, "How 'Religion' Came to Be Translated as 'Shūkyō,'" *Japan Review* 25 (2013): 89–111.

4 Kobayashi小林, *日本人の宗教的意識や行動*.

5 Hannah Gould, *When Death Falls Apart: Making and Unmaking the Necromaterial Traditions of Contemporary Japan* (Chicago: Chicago University Press, 2023), 4–6.

6 Mitsuhashi Tadashi 三橋正, *平安時代の信仰と宗教儀礼* (東京: 続群書 類従完成会, 2000), 597.

7 Tamamuro Taijō 圭室諦成, *葬式仏教* (東京: 大法輪閣, 1979).

8 Agency for Cultural Affairs 文化庁, *宗教年鑑*.

9 Richard Jaffe, "Meiji Religious Policy, Sōtō Zen and the Clerical Marriage Problem, " *Japanese Journal of Religious Studies* 25, nos. 1–2 (1998): 45–85.

10 Jacqueline I. Stone and Mariko N. Walter, "Introduction," *Death and the Afterlife in Japanese Buddhism*, ed. Jacqueline I. Stone and Mariko N. Walter (Honolulu: University of Hawai'i Press, 2009), 7.

11 Japan Consumer's Association 日本消費者協会, *第12回「葬儀についてのアンケート調査」報告書*, March 2023, 34.

12 Fujii Masao 藤井正雄, Hanayama Shōyū 花山勝友, and Nakano Tōzen 中野東禅, *仏教葬祭大事典* (東京: 雄山閣, 1980).

13 Fujii 藤井, Hanayama 花山, and Nakano 中野, *仏教葬祭大事典*, 87–8.

14 Stephen Covell, "The Price of Naming the Dead: Posthumous Precept Names and Critiques of Contemporary Japanese Buddhism," in *Death and the Afterlife in Japanese Buddhism*, eds. Jacqueline I. Stone & Mariko N. Walter (Honolulu: University of Hawai'i Press, 2009), 293–324.

15 Ishii Kenji 石井研士, *データブック 現代日本人の宗教 増補改訂版* (東京: 新曜社, 2007), 76.

16 Hikaru Suzuki, *The Price of Death: The Funeral Industry in Contemporary Japan* (Stanford: Stanford University Press, 2000), 29.

17 Suzuki, *The Price of Death*, 27.

18 Japan Consumer's Association 日本消費者協会, *第12回「葬儀についてのアンケート調査」報告書*, 34.

19 Jinja Honchō Chōsabu 神社本庁調査部, ed., *神葬祭の栞* (東京: 神社本庁, 1970).

20 Timothy Benedict, *Spiritual Ends: Religion and the Heart of Dying in Japan* (California: University of California Press, 2022).

21 Japan Consumer's Association 日本消費者協会, *第12回「葬儀についてのアンケート調査」報告書*, 34.

22 Oriens Institute for Religious Research オリエンス宗教研究所, ed., *キリスト教葬儀のこころ* (東京: オリエンス宗教研究所, 2010), 122.

23 Hikita Hiroshi 疋田博, *キリスト教葬儀* (千葉: イーグレープ, 2005), 51.

24 Sōka Gakkai, "A Global Organization," accessed November 2, 2023, www.sokaglobal.org/about-the-soka-gakkai/at-a-glance/a-global-organization.html.

25 Sōka Gakkai 創価学会, "友人葬," *創価学会のお葬式*, 2023, www.sokagakkai.jp/w2/yujinsou/.

6   The Funeral Industry

6.1 The History and Present of the Funeral Industry

The origins of the Japanese funeral industry date back to the latter half of the 17th century, with manufacturers of ritual goods for funeral processions, known as *ganshi* (龕師). The term *gan* (龕) refers to the coffin that holds a body, or to a covering for that coffin.[1] *Ganshi* manufactured, sold, and occasionally rented coffins and the palanquins used to carry them, as well as various ritual goods used in funeral processions (see Section 6.1.1.).[2] *Ganshi* had various alternative names, including *gan* merchants (龕屋 *ganya*), vehicle makers (乗物屋 *norimonoya*), and coffin makers (棺屋 *hitsugiya*). When organising a funeral, families engaged such suppliers to procure ritual implements and hired palanquin bearers from manual labour contractors to perform the funeral procession.

In the Meiji period (1868–1912), businesses offering goods and labour contracts for funeral processions emerged, and they came to be known as "funeral companies" (葬儀社 *sōgisha*).[3] After the Taishō period (1912–1926), in large cities such as Tokyo, processions were replaced by ceremonies, and the business of funeral companies expanded to include the decoration of the ceremony venue, encoffining, and registration of the death.[4] After WWII, funeral ceremonies also became popular in rural areas, with altars and floral displays used nationwide. The funeral industry subsequently spread throughout the country and in urban areas, funeral company workers came to officiate ceremonies.[5] In the 1980s, funeral companies started to own ceremony halls and take on the role of comprehensive service provision. In recent years, funeral companies have positioned themselves within the care industry and expanded their service offerings.

DOI: 10.4324/9781003451914-6

This includes non-religious farewell parties and funerals, family-only funerals, and one-day and direct funerals (Section 7.1.)

When organising a funeral in Japan, it is now entirely normal to engage the services of a funeral company. The funeral company collects the dead, prepares and encoffins the body, and plans the ceremony in line with the bereaved's wishes and any particular feelings of the deceased. While supporting the bereaved family, they begin preparations for the funeral (Section 7.2.2). They make the reservation at the crematorium, engage the florist to prepare a floral altar, engage a caterer to provide food at the wake and post-funeral dinner, order thank-you gifts from gift companies, and reserve a hearse. In recent years, the services offered by funeral companies have widened further, to include services like funeral pre-planning and the purchase of graves and altars.

6.2 Regulatory Frameworks

6.2.1 Funeral Companies

In Japan, businesses that offer funerals are generally referred to as "the funeral industry" (葬儀業 *sōgigyō*), but historically, this sector has also been known more specifically as "the funeral ceremony industry" (葬祭業 *sōsaigyō*).[6] Under the Japan Standard Industrial Classification (日本標準産業分類), which is one of the statistical standards of the Ministry of Internal Affairs and Communications, this industry sits within the major category "N Life-related service industries, entertainment industry", and the sub-category "79 Other life-related service industries", and sub-category "796 Ceremonial Occasions Businesses", and it is divided into "7961 Funeral Industry", "7962 Wedding Hall Business" and "7963 Ceremonial Mutual Aid Associations".[7]

There are multiple types of business within this classification. Firstly, funeral companies that specialize in the provision of funeral services. Secondly, mutual aid associations for ceremonies, more specifically the funeral departments of companies that perform both weddings and funerals. Thirdly, agricultural cooperatives, which are complex businesses with a distinctive structure that sometimes offer funeral services alongside many other services. The market split is approximately 50% specialized funeral companies, 40% mutual aid associations, and 8% agricultural cooperatives.[8]

No official permission or registration is required to open a funeral business in Japan. Therefore, it is not possible to ascertain the exact number of such companies currently operating. In terms of sales, the largest funeral company currently operating in Japan is Bellco, which is a mutual aid association (Section 6.2.1) offering funeral and wedding services. Bellco did 545 million yen in sales in the financial year 2022–23.[9] The second largest company is Nihon Ceremony, and the third largest is Ceremoa. Bellco is also the largest mutual aid association in Japan, with over 2.5 million members. The company owns two hotels, 30 wedding halls, six wedding chapels, five styling studios, and 243 multipurpose function halls, and organises approximately 40,000 funerals per year.[10]

6.2.2 Funeral Directors

There is no mandatory qualification or licensing system for funeral service providers. The Funeral Director Skill Examination (葬祭ディレクター技能審査) is a voluntary examination, and it is possible to work in the industry without it. The Funeral Director Skill Examination was established by the National Japan Funeral Service Cooperative Association (全日本葬祭業協同組合連合会), an industry association for funeral companies, and the National Japan Ceremony Mutual Aid Association (全日本冠婚葬祭互助協会), an industry association for ceremonial mutual aid associations, who made a joint request to the then Ministry of Labor (currently, the Ministry of Health, Labor and Welfare) to establish a qualification certification system. Through this request, the "Funeral Director Skills Examination Association" was established in 1995 and certified by the Ministry of Labor in March 1996.[11]

The purpose of this association is "to improve the knowledge and skills of people engaged in the funeral industry, as well as to improve their social status".[12] The Association offers two levels of qualification: Grade 1 and Grade 2. Grade 2 covers detailed knowledge and skills in funeral service provision including family meetings, venue setup, and ceremony design. Grade 1 includes and extends this knowledge to all different types of funerals, like company funerals, while Grade 2 only covers conventional funerals for families. The prerequisite for taking the Grade 2 exam is to have at least 2 years' experience of working in the funeral industry. Alternatively, those who have completed the prescribed curriculum of a funeral education institution (vocational school) that is certified by the Association receive advanced standing. Grade 1 is for those who have at least 5 years' experience working in the funeral industry, or those who have passed the Grade 2 exam before 2019 and have at least 2 years' work experience. There is a written test and a practical test for each grade. The tests assess skills like preparing incense for ritual offering, funeral arranging, and officiating.

Since the first examination was held in 1996, a total of approximately 37,000 Funeral Directors have been certified.[13] Although this is not a mandatory qualification, there is significant interest from the sector with more and more Funeral Directors becoming qualified. These qualifications not only provide customers with a sense of security, they also provide a means for workers to generate pride in their work, protect standards of professionalism, and gain recognition.[14]

6.3 Industry Organisations

6.3.1 Specialist Funeral Companies

Full-time funeral service providers range in type and size from large, publicly listed companies to small family-run businesses. In particular, there are a large number of small-scale businesses. Small- to medium-sized businesses are often passed down through the family line. Some offer services for pet cremations and funerals, however, this is almost entirely a separate industry.

The All Japan Funeral Directors Co-Operation (全日本葬祭業協同組合連合会) is a national industry organisation to which funeral companies belong. The organisation name is frequently abbreviated to *Zensōren*. This organisation was first established in 1956 as the National Japan Funeral Industry Association (全日本葬祭業組合連合会) and became the All Japan Funeral Directors Co-Operation or *Zensōren* in 1975.

The origins of the *Zensōren* date back to the wartime period. Under a wartime control directive, existing unions were dissolved and reorganized under the Commercial and Industrial Associations Act (商工組合法) of 1943. Funeral goods manufacturers and distributors became controlled associations, and wood for coffins, nails, paper, textiles, and other items could only be obtained through these associations.[15] In the post-war period, in the context of reconstruction efforts focused on improving the quality of living and the introduction of value added tax (VAT), trade associations in six major cities (Tokyo, Yokohama, Nagoya, Kyoto, Osaka, and Kobe) banded together. These trade associations played a central role in bringing business operators together, and in 1956 the National Japan Funeral Industry Association was established, with 13 unions initially joining.[16]

This unified trade association transitioned into an economic cooperative in the service industry, governed by the then Ministry of International Trade and Industry. In 1975, the All Japan Funeral Directors Co-Operation *(Zensōren)* was established, with 28 business cooperatives participating.[17] Today, *Zensōren* has 56 business cooperatives and 1,231 member companies nationwide, making it the largest association of funeral businesses in Japan. *Zensōren* are involved in administering government-commissioned surveys, organising disaster relief, and administering the Funeral Director Skills Examinations. *Zensōren* also offers various economic benefits to participating companies.[18] However, not all providers have elected to join.

6.3.2 Ceremonial Mutual Aid Associations

A ceremonial mutual aid association administers a system through which customers secure designated funeral and wedding services by paying a set amount in advance each month. While the terms 'mutual aid' and 'cooperative' have grassroots or anti-capitalist associations in English, this is primarily a business management strategy in Japan, one that raises funds from members to use as investment capital.[19]

Mutual aid associations for ceremonial occasions are businesses that require approval from the Ministry of Economy, Trade and Industry, under the Installment Sales Act, which mandates certain consumer protections. As of October 2022, there are 206 such associations operating nationwide.[20] In addition to funerals, these associations also provide services for weddings and other rites of passage, but since the 2000s, funerals have become their chief offering. The relevant industry association is the Japan Ceremonial Occasion Mutual Aid Society (一般社団法人全日本冠婚葬祭互助協会), a general incorporated association established in 1973. As of October 2022, it is comprised of 205 companies.[21]

This system was developed in 1948 by the Yokosuka City Mutual Aid Association for Ceremonies in Yokosuka City, Kanagawa Prefecture. Mutual aid associations rapidly spread in the 1960s, growing from 49 organisations in 1965 to 234 organisations in 1971.[22] At this time, mutual aid associations were also subject to greater regulation following the revision of the Installment Sales Act, which came to administer business licenses. The Japan Ceremonial Occasion Mutual Aid Society was established as a unified voice for the sector in response to this increased popularity and regulation.[23]

6.3.3 Agricultural Cooperatives

The Japan Agricultural Cooperatives (農業協同組合) or "JA" is a farmers' cooperative that was formed in 1947. The structure and kind of businesses within this cooperative are varied. They include businesses managed directly by agricultural cooperatives at the municipal level, businesses with private investors, businesses with multiple agricultural cooperatives that join together to form a management association, and various collaboratives with prefectural organisations. The number of funerals handled by agricultural cooperatives began to rapidly increase from the 1960s.[24] Although the target customer for these services is union members, it is often not limited to them. In rural areas, the uses of agricultural cooperatives within funeral services are vast. This includes some unique initiatives, such as building large funeral halls to accommodate large numbers of mourners and using agricultural products as gifts at funerals. In recent years, as funerals have become smaller, such initiatives have become rarer.

6.4 Related Industries

6.4.1 Hearse Industry

In Japan, the use of hearses and horse-drawn carriages dates back to the Taishō period, concurrent with the disappearance of funeral processions. At the time, hearses tended to be imported cars, but shrine-style (宮型 *miyagata*) hearses, with palanquin structures attached to the rear, were also manufactured and used.[25] The use of hearses spread nationwide after WWII. In addition to shrine-style hearses, undecorated vans and minibuses, which transport both the coffin and the mourners, began to be used. Western-style hearses entered Japan in the late 1980s. In recent years, an increasing number of crematoria have prohibited the entry of shrine-style hearses due to their conspicuous style. Such hearses also incur high maintenance costs.

Hearses are used to transport bodies and are legally classified as cargo transport vehicles. In 1990, the Freight Vehicle Transportation Business Law (貨物自動車運送事業法) was enacted and the hearse transportation business was liberalised from a license system to a permit system. Under 2003 legal reforms, hearse fee schedules could be submitted to the government after, not before, being set by industry and freight rates also become more liberal.[26] The hearse industry organisation is the National Hearse Automobile Association (一般社団法人全国霊柩自動車協会), a general incorporated association, and its members are hearse automobile associations in each prefecture, with businesses from 43 prefectures currently participating[27].

6.4.2 *Mortuary Industry*

In Japanese, embalming is described as "corpse sanitation preservation" (遺体衛生保全 *itai eisei hozen*). In the past, embalming was only carried out at select medical universities. However, in 1988, the first embalming centre for the funeral industry was established in Saitama Prefecture. At that time, embalmers who had obtained qualifications in the United States of America or Canada were employed. In 1994, the International Funeral Science Association in Japan (日本遺体衛生保全協会) was established and began to set its own standards. Later, a vocational school was established and embalmers began to be trained in Japan.[28] In contemporary Japan, the advertised benefits of embalming include hygiene, preservation, and restoration. The Japanese translation of this term emphasizes public health, although meanings of restoration and peaceful death appear equally important to bereaved families.[29]

In the past, funeral service providers carried out encoffining and body preparations. But in recent years, specialty mortuary service providers, known as "encoffiners" (納棺師 *nōkanshi*), have emerged. They provide services including washing, dressing, makeup, and hair styling. In the late 1980s, ritual corpse bathing (湯灌 *yukan*) companies also emerged and have become a nationwide industry. This is a service that uses a mobile nursing care bathing system to cleanse the dead body[30] (Section 7.2.2). In its marketing, this modern industry aligns itself with traditional folk practices of families bathing the dead.

6.4.3 Floristry and Artificial Floristry Industries

As flowers are an integral part of modern Japanese funeral ceremonies, funeral companies cultivate strong connections with florists. Some floristry companies sell funeral flowers alongside their main business, while others specialize in funeral flowers.[31] Today, fresh flowers are used for the funeral altar (Section 7.2.4) and other decorations for the coffin and venue. However, until the post-war period, artificial flowers were more popular, and in some regions, fresh flowers were never used. Artificial lotus flowers were popular during the Meiji period. As artificial flower wreaths became more and more popular, they grew in size, and slowly, the central void was also filled with flowers, resulting in a 'disk shape' for floral displays that is common in Japan today. During the period of high economic growth postwar, such wreaths became popular throughout the country, with multiple wreaths displayed in homes and at funerals. However, since the 1990s, wreaths have fallen out of fashion.

Fresh flowers were also used in the Meiji period, particularly for arranging flowers and foliage in bamboo vases. Gradually this morphed into flowers arranged in baskets and placed before the deceased as an offering. Artificial electric lighting at night made it possible to control the blooming of flowers, particularly chrysanthemums, which could thus be supplied year round. It is for this reason that chrysanthemums became the most commonly used flower at Japanese funerals.[32] Chrysanthemums also have a number of symbolic associations that tie them to death: they are white (the colour of mourning in Japan) and have a scent reminiscent of incense. They are also associated with wealth and dignity in Japan, as they are the emblem of the imperial crest.

A fresh flower altar (生花祭壇 *seikasaidan*) was arguably used for the first time at Prime Minister Shigeru Yoshida's state funeral in 1967. Afterwards, fresh flower altars began to be used for group funerals such as company funerals. Since the 1990s, elaborate fresh flower altars with intricate designs incorporating many hundreds if not thousands of flowers have become more and more popular.

Notes

1 The term *gan* originally referred to the reliquary that housed a Buddhist statue. As in Buddhist funerals, the dead is ritually transformed into a Buddha, the term *gan* was also applied to the coffin for the dead.
2 Kinoshita Mitsuo　木下光男, *近世三昧聖と葬送文化* (東京: 塙書房, 2010).
3 Inoue Shōichi 井上章一, *霊柩車の誕生* (東京:朝日新聞社, 1984).
4 Murakami Kōkyō 村上興匡,"大正期東京における葬送儀礼の変化と近代化," *宗教研究* 64, no.1 (1990): 37–61.
5 Yamada Shinya 山田慎也, *現代日本の死と葬儀: 葬祭業の展開と死生観の変容* (東京:東京大学出版会, 2007).
6 Tamagawa　Takako　玉川貴子,　*葬儀業界の戦後史*　(東京:青弓社, 2018),13.
7 Ministry of Internal Affairs and Communications 総務省, "日本標準産業分類," accessed January 30, 2024, www.soumu.go.jp/toukei_toukatsu/index/seido/sangyo/H25index.htm.
   The current Japanese Standard Industrial Classification was the 13th revised edition, published October 2013. The 14th revised version was published in June 2023, and will come into effect from April 2024, but there are no changes regarding the funeral industry.
8 Tamagawa 玉川,葬儀業界の戦後史,13.
9 Gyōkai Dōkō Search　業界動向サーチ, "葬儀業界の動向や現状、ランキングなどを解説," January 21, 2024, accessed February 27, 2024, https://gyokai-search.com/3-sougi.html
10 Bellco　ベルコ, "About," accessed February 27, 2024, www.bellco.co.jp/about
11 Tanaka Daisuke 田中大介, *葬儀業のエスノグラフィー* (東京: 東京大学出版会, 2017).
12 Funeral Director Skills Examination Association, "葬祭ディレクター技能審査," accessed January 29, 2024, www.sousai-director.jp/.
13 Ibid. The examination was suspended temporarily in 2020 due to Covid-19.
14 Tanaka 田中, 葬儀業のエスノグラフィー, 75.
15 Zensōren Nijūgonenshi Hensan Iinkai　全葬連二十五年史編纂委員会　(ed.),　全葬連二十五年史　(東京: 全日本葬祭業協同組合連合会, 1982): 90–91.
16 Ibid., 94–97.
17 Ibid., 118–124.
18 All Japan Funeral Directors Co-Operation, "全葬連の概要," accessed January　30,　2024,　www.zensoren.or.jp/zensoren/zensoren_gaiyou_01.html.
19 Tanaka 田中, *葬儀業のエスノグラフィー*, 56.

20 Japan Ceremonial Occasion Mutual Aid Society, "互助協会とは," accessed January 30, 2024, www.zengokyo.or.jp/about/zengokyo/greeting/.

21 Ibid.

22 Syadanhōjin Zen'nihon Kankonsōsai Gojokyōkai Jūgosyūnen Kinenjigyō Tokubetsuhensan Iinkai 社団法人全日本冠婚葬祭互助協会十五周年記念事業特別委員会, ed. 冠婚葬祭互助会四十年の歩み (東京: 社団法人全日本冠婚葬祭互助協会, 1989).

23 Ibid.

24 Kamakura Shinsho 鎌倉新書, 葬儀白書 (1997), 78–9.

25 Inoue 井上, 霊柩車の誕生.

26 Himon'ya Hajime 碑文谷創, 葬儀概論 増補三訂版 (東京: 葬祭ディレクター技能審査協会, 2011), 337.

27 Japan Hearse Association, "組織," accessed January 30, 2024, www.09net.jp/about.html#b

28 International Funeral Science Association in Japan, "組織案内," accessed January 30, 2024, www.embalming.jp/organization/.

29 Yamada Shinya 山田慎也, "越境する葬儀: 日本におけるエンバーミング," in 現代民俗誌の地平 I 越境, ed. Shinohara Tōru (東京: 朝倉書店, 2003), 35–53.

30 Suzuki Hikaru, *The Price of Death* (Stanford: Stanford University Press, 2000), 154–157.

31 Tanaka 田中, 葬儀業のエスノグラフィー, 79.

32 Yamada Shinya 山田慎也, "葬送儀礼における供花と菊の利用," 葬送文化 18 (2016): 13–25.

7　The Funeral

7.1　Funeral Types

7.1.1　From Funeral Procession to Farewell Ceremony

From the end of the Middle Ages, in parallel with the spread of the household (家 *ie*) system among the common people and the temple-parishioner system (檀家制度 *danka seido*) that bound these households to temples, Buddhist rituals for the dead became common (Chapter 2).[1] It is under these conditions that the basic format of Japanese Buddhist funerals emerged. Although there are differences and exceptions depending on the teachings of each Buddhist school, the basic principle governing funerals in Japan is that the dead are treated as disciples of the Buddha: they take precepts and they are guided toward Buddhahood and/or to the Pure Land.[2] The rite became systematised with the repetition of rituals accompanying the funeral procession (葬列 *sōretsu*), being the transport of the dead body from spaces of living (their home) to spaces of the dead (temples, cemeteries, and crematoria).[3] Historically, these rituals included the chanting of sutras at the deathbed, bathing the dead in warm water (湯灌 *yukan*), encoffining, and wake. The next day was the ceremonial start to the funeral procession, including rituals for sending off the coffin and then guiding the afterlife journey of the deceased (引導作法 *indō sahō*) performed at the temple, cemetery, and crematorium, followed by burial or cremation. The procession itself was greatly emphasised in these rituals as not simply a mode of transport, but a symbolic journey from this world to the next.

Since the Taishō period (1912–1926), funeral processions were gradually abolished in large cities such as Tokyo, and funeral services

DOI: 10.4324/9781003451914-7

Figure 7.1 Funeral Procession, Taishō Era. Photograph from personal collection of Shinya Yamada (author).

or 'farewell ceremonies' (告別式) began to be held instead (Section 2.3.3).[4] Furthermore, funeral ceremonies were held not only at temples and funeral parlours, but also in private homes. After World War II and the subsequent period of high economic growth, funeral processions and farewell ceremonies became increasingly integrated and spread throughout the country as distinct, but conjoined, rites. Gradually, the farewell ceremony replaced the procession as the central funeral rite. As these ceremonies became more popular, specialty funeral altars (葬儀祭壇 *sōgi saidan*) were erected in homes and ceremony halls as the locus of ritual activity. The work of Funeral Directors expanded to include setting up the altar and handling bodies (Chapter 6).

7.1.2 Conventional Funerals (Ippansō)

This model, of decorating an altar and holding wakes, rituals, and farewell ceremonies before it, became popular nationwide in the period of post-war economic growth. It is recognisable today as a 'conventional funeral'(一般葬 *ippansō*), and described in detail in Section 7.2. During this period, cremation also became more popular, rising to over 99.97% of the population today.[5] Regional variations exist in the timing of the cremation and funeral. In most of Japan, cremation follows the funeral. However, in regions such as Tōhoku, Kantō, Chūbu, and Southern Kinki, where there is a historic tradition of whole body burial, cremation is sometimes performed before the funeral ceremony. Cremated remains, rather than a corpse, are thus present at the funeral ceremony. This is called a *kotsusō* (骨葬) or 'bone funeral' and does not include a viewing of the body. In many areas of the Tōhoku region, when a person dies, they are cremated one to two days later, followed by a wake and funeral, and the cremated remains are interred on the same day. In some regions of the Kantō, Chūbu, and Kinki regions, cremation is performed the morning after the wake but before the funeral service. This mimics the traditional ritual process associated with whole body earth burials in these regions, whereby the funeral leads immediately to burial, concluding ritual practice at the graveside. In order to replicate this structure within the context of cremation, cremated remains must be made ready for interment immediately after the funeral (without the delays of travelling to the crematorium and waiting for cremation).

7.1.3 Family Funerals (Kazokusō)

In the 1990s, funerals began to become smaller and simpler. Previously, unlike weddings, attendees at Japanese funerals were not individually invited, but rather it was customary for those acquainted with the deceased to attend the funeral upon hearing of a death or reading public notices posted about funeral services. However, in the 1990s, there emerged cases of funerals being held in secret, with only a limited number of attendees and with no public notice posted about the death. At the time, such funerals were called 'secret funerals' (密葬 *missō*).[6] In some cases, even after learning of a death, people declined to attend the funeral. In the past, secret funerals were also performed when the death was considered shameful, taboo, or covert, such as suicides and funerals associated with organised crime.[7] In the 1990s, this changed as secret funerals began to be held for people of relatively high social status, including celebrities. Still, as secret funerals were performed in a clandestine manner, they retained negative associations.

This negative image of restricted funeral attendance has been recuperated in recent years through their positive rebranding as 'family funerals' (家族葬 *kazokusō*). Family funerals conjure an image of an intimate service without the presence of unrelated parties, and this term and practice have begun to gain wide social recognition in Japan. However, there is no set definition of what a 'family funeral' entails, including whether or not the death should be publicly announced, or the number and relation of people who may attend. There is thus broad variation, and in some cases, family funerals appear no different to conventional ones.[8] The rise in smaller funerals is attributed to people's desire for greater personalisation, but also serious challenges raised by Japan's demographics, including a declining birth rate, ageing population, and transition to a nuclear family structure. In contemporary Japan, many of the deceased are elderly and die with fewer living descendants, younger relatives, or friends to attend their funerals.[9]

7.1.4 Direct Funerals and One-day Funerals

Since the 2000s, instead of holding wakes, funerals, and memorial services separately, simplified funeral rites have become popular. These include 'direct funerals' (直葬 *chokusō* or *jikisō*) and 'one-day funerals' (一日葬 *ichinichisō*).

At a 'direct funeral', the body is cremated without rituals including the wake, ceremony, or memorial service. After death, the body is transferred to the mortuary of a funeral home, crematorium, or body storage facility and then cremated 24 hours later. If close relatives choose to be present, they may undertake a final viewing and farewell of the deceased at the crematorium. Sometimes, a simple religious ritual such as a priest chanting a sutra may also be performed. This form of funeral service has rapidly increased since 2000 and is estimated to comprise approximately 20 to 30% of funerals in Tokyo and around 10% nationwide.[10]

A one-day funeral is a condensation of funerary rituals that would normally be expected to take at least two days, by eliminating the wake and just holding a funeral ceremony before cremation.[11] Conventionally, the wake stands alone as separate ritual and may attract more attendees than the funeral ceremony. By eliminating the wake, this format condenses the number of attendees and the number of rituals to one event. One-day funerals were already popular in

Tokyo before 2020, but with the outbreak of Covid-19, people were encouraged to avoid eating and drinking at public events like wakes, and so this funeral format spread nationwide.

7.2 The Funeral Process

7.2.1 Deathbed Rituals

In contemporary Japan, hospitals are the primary place of death, with rising numbers of deaths at aged care homes. In this situation, doctors are responsible for confirming death and issuing a Death Certificate (Section 4.2.1.). If a person dies in a hospital or another institution, a nurse will likely clean the body. In the past, if the family were at the bedside at the time of death, they would leave the room during the washing. However, in recent years, it has become more common for family members to participate in certain preparations, including washing the body and applying postmortem makeup. Bereaved families are directed to organise transport for the deceased's body as soon as possible, even during the middle of the night or on a public holiday, as hospitals do not keep the deceased in the mortuary for extended periods. Sometimes, postmortem treatment is completed in the hospital bed and the body is transported directly from the room. For this reason, funeral companies are available around the clock. Bereaved families need to engage a funeral company promptly. In the past, funeral companies were attached to hospitals and were recommended to families. It was possible for families to choose another, independent, provider, but in principle, most went with the default choice. At hospitals and other institutions, doctors and nurses are often present when funeral company staff arrive to take possession of the deceased's body. As a sign of respect to the deceased and the bereaved, staff often see off the transport vehicle with a deep bow.

7.2.2 Funeral Preparations

7.2.2.1 Laying Out

In the past, the deceased's body was often transported from the hospital to their former home. Today, the deceased is typically transported to the funeral company's mortuary facility. Because of the high number of deaths in cities like Tokyo, the body may alternatively be stored at the mortuary facility of a transport company or crematorium.

At home, the body is laid out on a futon on the tatami floor. The white sheet used to transport the body from the hospital is spread out on top of the futon as a sheet. Beside the pillow, a candlestick, incense burner, and a vase are placed on a plain wooden table as decorations (枕飾り *makurakazari*). In the vase, a single flower, white chrysanthemum, or birch branch is arranged. The candle and incense are lit.[12] In the past, candles and incense remained lit throughout the entire period of the wake. Next, rice and dumplings are arranged as offerings. These are known as 'pillow rice' (枕飯 *makurameshi*) and 'pillow dumplings' (枕団子 *makuradango*) because they are arranged beside the head of the deceased. The rice is shaped into a mound and the chopsticks are inserted vertically (this arrangement is considered taboo in everyday life). The dumplings vary in shape and number depending on the region, but in the Tokyo area, six round dumplings are served. If the deceased is stored in a mortuary facility, these offerings may be prepared by the funeral company, but are often not made.

Figure 7.2 Offerings of rice and dumplings made to the deceased. Photograph by Shinya Yamada (author).

7.2.2.2 Funeral Meeting

The funeral meeting takes place at home or at the funeral company. During this meeting, the bereaved family have many decisions to make, including the designation of 'chief mourner' (喪主 *moshu*), the funeral schedule, venue, religious elements and format, the type of coffin, the type of floral altar, the meal, gifts for attendees, and more. In the past, these decisions would have been made by the neighbourhood associations who organised funerals, the head of the family line, or the company where the deceased or chief mourner was employed. Furthermore, previously, the chief mourner was always the male head of the family. But in recent years, the wife often takes on the role of chief mourner when her husband dies. If the deceased has only female children, then in the past, the daughter's husband would be designated chief mourner, but today, it is often the daughter herself. Finally, in recent years, funeral scheduling has become more challenging, with increased demands on the time of the crematorium, officiating priest, and funeral home.

7.2.2.3 Funeral Venue

One crucial decision is the selection of the funeral venue. Most funerals are held in halls located at funeral companies, mutual aid associations, or some renovated crematoria. In busy metropolitan areas like Tokyo, in order to maximise usage, many funeral companies have implemented a 24-hour hiring period for venues. The changeover time is around 3pm each day. Preparations for the wake begin from this time, and the wake starts at 6 to 7pm and ends at 9pm. The funeral service is held the next day for about one hour from 10 or 11am, followed by the cremation at 12pm, during which time the attendees have a meal together, then collect the remains, and finally disband.

Home funerals are generally decreasing but continue in some regions of Japan as in the past. In other regions, wakes continue to be held in the home while the funeral has moved from a Buddhist temple to a funeral company. There are also a small number of simple home funerals with only family in attendance. The body is laid out at home, a priest attends to chant sutras, and then the body is sent to the crematorium.

7.2.2.4 Washing and Encoffining

The encoffining of the body is often completed on the morning of or day before the wake. In some regions of Japan, it takes place after the wake, but this has become less common. In the past, the rite of *yukan* (湯灌), in which the body is ritually cleansed in water, was performed before this step. This rite used what is called "inverted water" (逆さ水 *sakasa mizu*), where hot water is added to cold water to adjust the temperature (in reverse of usual practice). The body was then placed in the tub and washed. This type of corpse bathing was practiced in urban areas until around the Taishō period (1912–1926) and continued in rural areas after WWII in the case of deaths at home. However, this tradition has slowly disappeared as people die in hospital.[13]

Funeral Directors were first responsible for cleaning the hands and feet of the deceased, placing them in the coffin, and applying makeup. Later this role was taken over by companies specialising in mortuary work and *yukan*. In particular, in the late 1980s, specialised *yukan* companies (湯灌業者 *yukan gyōsha*) devised a method of washing corpses modelled on bathing services for home nursing care and this came to be synonymous with *yukan*.[14] This *yukan* method is a performance, with the body placed in a mobile bathtub in between the bereaved family and staff. Staff place a long towel over the body and wash the body beneath the towel, so that the deceased's bare skin is never visible to the bereaved. The bereaved can also participate by washing the hands, feet, hair, or other exposed parts of the body. Additionally, since 1988, embalming has been performed on members of the general public in Japan. If the bereaved choose embalming, the process is carried out as soon as possible at a specialist embalmer's facility, and then the body in placed in the coffin and returned to the home or funeral company. Embalming is not a widespread practice in Japan. In 2022, 70,596 bodies were embalmed, which represent about 4.5% of total deaths that year.[15]

After cleansing, the deceased is dressed in fresh clothes. Traditionally, a white kimono of light fabric, known as *shirokatabira* (白帷子), is preferred. When dressing the dead, the kimono is draped in the opposite way to when dressing the living, such that the left collar of the kimono lays closest to the chest (左前 *hidarimae*). The obi belt is tied in a vertical knot, which is also unique to funerals. Other items of clothing mimic the costume of a Buddhist pilgrim and prepare the dead for their posthumous journey. A bag, known as *zudabukuro* (頭陀袋) and similar to what Buddhists priests use, is hung around the deceased's neck, and filled with keepsakes including six coins. These coins (六文銭 *rokumonsen* or 六道銭 *rokudōsen*), are a denomination of small change from the early modern period. They serve as an offering to the six Jizō Boddhisatva and/or as a fare for crossing the mythical Sanzu River, which the deceased are said to traverse on their journey through the afterlife (broadly analogous to the River Styx). Today, because crematoria do not allow metal objects to be placed in the coffin, paper copies of the coins are used instead. Further, fabric arm guards (手甲 *tekkō*) and leg guards (脚半 *kyahan*) are wrapped around the deceased's hands and feet. In the past, a large white triangle of fabric or paper, known as *hitai eboshi* (額烏帽子) or *tenkan* (天冠), was tied around the forehead of the deceased. This headdress is often seen in depictions of ghosts in Japanese popular culture. A braided straw hat (編笠 *amigasa*) is also placed at the beside, and today, the white triangle headdress is often placed with the hat, rather than worn. Additionally, the deceased may hold a cane in their hand.

Traditionally, these white clothes were hurriedly sewn by family members or neighbours. The bleached fabric is torn by hand rather

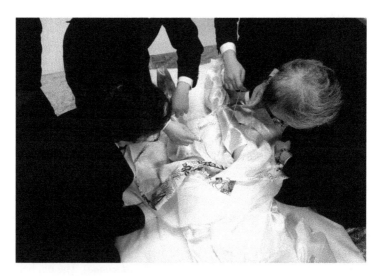

Figure 7.3 Family and funeral professionals assist in tying ceremonial leg guards to the deceased. Licensed image (Contributor: corosukechan3).

than cut with scissors and left with unfinished edges. The kimono is sewn together by multiple people, with each sleeve attached by a different person. These techniques are all considered taboo when sewing a regular kimono. Some families eschew this white clothing in favour of the deceased's finest kimono or a simple (colourful) yukata. In recent years, it has also become more common to dress the deceased in everyday wear. Especially when embalming is performed, the bereaved family may leave washing and dressing to professionals. And if dressing the body is difficult due the onset of rigor mortis, these adornments may simply be placed atop the body.

The body is then placed in the coffin. The futon is placed on the floor of the coffin and the quilt is arranged over the body. Dry ice is packed into the coffin to preserve the body. Depending on the weather and the condition of the body, if properly managed, it is possible for viewings to occur over the course of a week without any major deterioration. In general, coffins used in Japan are made of wood, and range from simple boxes constructed from hinoki, cypress, or paulownia, to elaborately decorated coffins. The style and shape of coffins has changed throughout time in concert with burial and cremation technologies. Today, almost all Japanese coffins have a small window with a set of double-doors, located around the head of the deceased, which are opened at the crematorium to allow mourners to view the face of the deceased and say a final goodbye.

7.2.3 The Wake

The wake was originally an occasion for those close to the deceased to pass the night together. Indeed, in Japanese, the term wake, *tsuya* (通夜), is composed of two characters that literally mean 'pass the night'. It is also known as *togi* (伽), literally, 'nursing' or 'attending'. During the liminal phase between life and death, the wake was a time to pray for the repose of the soul and the dead's happiness in the afterlife. Buddhist priests would read sutras and local religious groups (念仏講 *nenbutsukō*) would chant mantras. Participants would stay awake all night with candles and incense sticks alight and would partake in midnight snacks.

The general format of the wake in contemporary Japan retains these major characteristics and rituals: friends, family, and religious officials attend, prayers and sutras are chanted, offerings of incense, candles, and flowers are placed before the deceased, and the chief

Figure 7.4 A typical Japanese coffin, with small windows positioned at the face of the deceased.

mourner gives a speech to close the event. In the past, wakes were only attended by close relatives and friends, but during the post-war period, co-workers and other acquaintances who could not attend the funeral service the following day started attending wakes. Gradually, people began to attend wakes as an alternative to the funeral ceremony. In the late 20th century, the number of people attending wakes far outweighed the number of people attending the funeral, at times three to one.

The wake meal, which originated simply as a midnight snack, has gradually evolved to become an elaborate dinner party. Until the early 1980s, even in more liberal regions like Tokyo, the cuisine served at the wake was limited to simple monastic food (精進料理 *shōjin ryōri*), including simmered vegetables, tempura, and sushi. This tradition of *shōjin ryōri* derives from Buddhist teachings that forbid killing living creatures. In the immediate bereavement period, families forgo eating fish or meat in order to generate merit and send the dead to the

Pure Land. However, these taboos have slowly weakened and raw fish dishes and even meat have become increasingly popular at wakes.

Further, rather than hosting a full wake in which people stay up all night, it has become common to host a 'half wake'(半通夜 *hantsuya*), at which all of the lights are extinguished momentarily to signal the completion of the event. Additionally, when hosting a wake at a funeral company, the use of open flames for candles and incense is increasingly restricted due to fire safety concerns. Since the downsizing and simplification of funerals in the 1990s, the number of one-day funerals without a wake has also increased. Communal dining at wakes and other events was also banned under restrictions related to the Covid-19 pandemic.

7.2.4 The Funeral (Sōgi) and Farewell Ceremony (Kokubetsushiki)

The central ritual is the funeral, which in modern times takes the form of a farewell ceremony. Strictly, the funeral (sōgi) is a religious ritual, and the farewell ceremony (kokubetsushiki) is a social ritual. While they were once considered separate events, today they are integrated. Funeral and farewell ceremonies vary depending on the religion and

Figure 7.5 Funeral altar (葬儀祭壇 *sōgi saidan*). Licensed image (Contributor: akiyoko).

religiosity of the organiser. The duration of most funerals is 40 minutes to an hour. The ceremony usually takes place before a funeral altar (葬儀祭壇 *sōgi saidan*), which is typically constructed from intricately carved, unvarnished wood and decorated with (often elaborate) floral displays, a memorial photograph and mortuary tablet (Chapter 11), and various religious implements. When the funeral is conducted at home, the bereaved family usually sit in the front with other attendees behind. When the funeral is conducted at a funeral parlour, this configuration may be reproduced, or the bereaved family may sit to the right of the funeral altar with other attendees to the left.

Today, most ceremonies consist of opening remarks, the recitation of sutras by Buddhist priests, and burning of incense by relatives and general attendees. At modern funerals, the opening and officiating is often entrusted to an employee of the funeral home. The ritual performance by priests is considered to be the core part of the ceremony. It is when the dead are posthumously ordained as Buddhist priests and given instruction to prepare them for their posthumous journey. These rites bookend by the chanting of Buddhist sutras. When this happens, the chief mourner and then close relatives are invited up to the funeral altar to burn incense. Afterwards, general mourners are invited forward to burn incense. The chanting of sutras continues until all mourners retake their seats. Once the incense burning and sutra chanting have finished, religious officials may depart the funeral.

The reading of the messages of condolence, from those unable to attend the service, takes place before or after the burning of incense. If a eulogy (弔辞 *chōji*) is given, it is conducted before the burning of incense, most likely by the chief mourner. This is a short speech that is often addressed directly to the dead and typically contains expressions of love and respect, as well as shared memories. After these messages, the officiant announces the final farewell part of the ceremony. The coffin is moved to the centre of the room. Fresh flowers are placed into the coffin. People may also place items of the deceased's personal belongings or keepsakes in the coffin. In the past, a tray of rice and dumplings were left on the grave at the cemetery on the day of the funeral and subsequent burial. However, with the introduction of cremation and difficulties in securing a grave, such that interment of cremated remains is often delayed, these offerings are now placed inside the coffin. Finally, the next of kin places the most luxurious flowers, such as rare orchids, into the coffin and closes the lid. At this stage, until the 2010s, it was common practice for a nail to be driven into the corner of the coffin. By tradition, the nail was hit with a stone rather than a hammer. However, this custom has all but disappeared in cities.

When the coffin closes, the chief mourner or family representative greets attendees. As a legacy of the funeral procession tradition, there is a set order and roles for mourners when transporting the deceased from the funeral to crematorium. As the coffin is removed, the chief mourner follows carrying the mortuary tablet and the next closest relative carries a photograph of the deceased. The coffin is loaded into a hearse and driven to the crematorium. The chief mourner often sits in the passenger seat of the hearse, and others head to the crematorium by private car. Generally, only close relatives continue to the crematorium, with the general attendees returning home. There are various regional traditions that accompany the departure of the hearse, such as breaking rice bowls or honking car horns.

Appropriate dress for wakes, funerals, and memorial services is referred to as *mofuku* (喪服). Although it depends on one's relationship to the deceased, in general, men wear a black kimono and hakama (Japanese style) or a business suit (Western style), while women wear a black kimono (Japanese style) or black dress (Western style). Children often wear their school uniform. At Buddhist funerals, mourners commonly carry a string of prayer beads (数珠 *juzu*). In the past, mourning clothes consisted of white kimono, the same as for weddings. However, since the Meiji era (1868–1912), when Western ceremonial dress was introduced, black mourning clothes have become the norm. These standards of dress may be relaxed at informal, non-religious funerals.

7.2.5 At the Crematorium

Upon arrival at the crematorium, the coffin is removed from the hearse to a trolley and transported to the funeral room, or directly to the pre-cremator hall (炉前ホール) (Section 9.1.4). It is common for there then to be a final moment of farewell between the deceased and the living, via the small window in the coffin. The coffin is then wheeled to the cremator. Buddhist priests in attendance chant short sutras and burn incense before or after this final goodbye.

Attendees wait in the designated rest area until the cremation is complete. During this time, sake and snacks are served as a respite, followed by rice balls and simple bento boxes at lunchtime. However, as cremation technology has become more efficient, the waiting time at crematorium has reduced, and meals are thus generally now limited. Funeral halls attached to crematoria in Tokyo and surrounding metropolitan areas increasingly hold funerals in the morning followed by the cremation, during which time attendees share lunch, as an alternative to the post-funeral dinner. After the cremation is complete, mourners participate in the bone raising ceremony (拾骨 *shūkotsu*), described in Section 9.2. When leaving the crematorium, the chief mourner carries the urn of cremated remains, which is placed in a wooden box with silk brocade coverings. The next of kin carry the memorial tablet and photo of the deceased.

7.2.6 *Memorial Service and Dinner*

Once the cremation is complete, the remains are stored (in the grave or temporarily at home) and memorial services are held. These services, called *an'i fugin* (安位諷経), *kankotsu gongyō* (還骨勤行) or *age* (アゲ), signify that the funeral has come to an end. They were commonly performed on the seventh day after a death, known as the "first seven-day memorial service" (初七日 *shonanoka*). However, from the 1980s, for ease and expediency, the first seven-day memorial service was brought forward and held on the same day as the funeral.[16] The number of people who attend memorial services varies by region. In places like Tokyo and Osaka, memorial services are usually attended by those who went to the crematorium, while in the Tōhoku region, people receive invitations for these services before the funeral.

After the memorial service, there is a dinner, known variously as *shōjin otoshi* (精進落とし), *shōjin age* (精進揚げ), *shiage* (仕上げ), or *otoki* (御斎). Although this name designates an end to the period of immediate mourning and religious devotion (including adherence to taboos), today it has a stronger meaning as the dinner after the funeral. The meal also serves as an opportunity to show gratitude to priests and others who have assisted with the funeral. The food served tends to be elaborate bento boxes, and multiple toasts are made during the evening.

In recent years, in Tokyo and other surrounding prefectures, the first seven-day memorial service has been held immediately following the funeral (*kuriage shonanoka* 繰上げ初七日). In this case, the memorial service consists of a brief sutra chanting before the coffin departs, and the meal is held while waiting for the cremation to finish. After picking up the cremated remains, the mourners disband.

7.2.7 At Home

After the first seven-day memorial service and dinner, the funeral rites are said to be complete. A memorial service is sometimes held on the 35th day, in the fifth week, after death. There are different regional traditions to mark this event. For example, in the North-Western Kanto region, people make a special kind of sweet mochi (dumpling) with red bean paste, known as *botamochi* (ぼた餅), for this occasion. This bean paste is spread on to the soles of traditional grass sandals, which are tied to walking sticks and then offered at the gravesite. This is said to prevent the dead from slipping in their journey through the afterlife.

In recent years, there has emerged a trend of holding a memorial service and interring remains in a grave on the 49th day after death. This period from death until the 49th day is called *chūin* (中陰) or *chūyū* (中有) and is said to be the liminal period during which one's fate after death is decided. During the period leading up to this day, the cremated remains and mortuary tablets are stored at home, usually on a temporal altar (中陰檀 *chūin dan*). Until this day, there are many folk beliefs surrounding the spirit of the dead, including that they hide in dark corners of the home or hover around the roof. People may prepare 49 small mochi (or 48 small mochi and one large one) and take them to the family temple or share with funeral attendees. After the 49th day ceremony, the liminal period is over, and families often send out reciprocal gifts to acknowledge the condolence payments they received.

Notes

1 Katsuda Itaru 勝田至, ed., *日本葬制史* (東京: 吉川弘文館, 2012), 182–95.
2 Fujii Masao 藤井正雄, *祖先祭祀の儀礼構造と民俗* (東京: 弘文堂, 1993), 549.
 This is called a 'posthumous monk'. In the Jōdo Shinshū school of Buddhism, rebirth is promised by Amida Buddha and so there is no need to guide the deceased. The dead also do not take posthumous precepts.

3 Yamada Shinya 山田慎也, "葬儀の変化と死のイメージ," in 近代化の中の誕生と死, eds. Yamada Shinya 山田慎也 and National Museum of Japanese History 国立歴史民俗博物館 (東京: 岩田書院, 2013), 136–9.

4 Yamada 山田, "葬儀の変化と死のイメージ,", 149–50.

5 The Ministry of Health, Labour and Welfare (MHLW) 厚生労働省, "Report on Public Health Administration and Services FY2021," accessed December 20, 2023, www.e-stat.go.jp/stat-search/files?page=1&toukei=00450027&tstat=000001031469.

6 In addition, cremations performed before the official funeral of a famous person were also referred to as secret cremations.

7 Himonya Hajime 碑文谷創, 葬儀概論 増補三訂版 (東京: 葬祭ディレクター技能審査協会, 2011), 72.

8 For example, the funeral for former Prime Minister Shinzo Abe, who was shot and killed on 8th July 2022, was held at Zōjōji Temple in Tokyo, and branded a 'family funeral', with the wake on the 11th of July and the funeral service on the 12th July. Despite this branding, a large number of people attended and an honour guard was also dispatched.

9 Kotani Midori 小谷みどり, "新たな死の共同性," in 無縁社会の葬儀と墓, eds. Yamada Shinya 山田慎也 and Doi Hiroshi 土居浩 (東京: 吉川弘文館, 2022), 2–5.

10 Himon'ya Hajime 碑文谷創, 葬儀概論 増補三訂版.

11 Ibid, 72.

12 In some areas, such as Chōshi City in Chiba Prefecture and Iida City in Nagano Prefecture, people continue to treat the dead as if they were sick for up to a day after they draw their last breath, and then later light incense sticks to mark the death.

13 Hiraku Suzuki, *The Price of Death: The Funeral Industry in Contemporary Japan* (Stanford: Stanford University Press, 2000), 184–5.

14 Ibid, 186–8.

15 International Funeral Science Association in Japan 日本遺体衛生保全協会, accessed January 24, 2024, www.embalming.jp/embalming/medic/.

16 Himon'ya 碑文谷, 葬儀概論 増補三訂版.

8 Finances

8.1 Funeral costs

As of the 2020-21 financial year, the average cost of a funeral ceremony in Japan is estimated to be 1.12 million yen.[1] This figure is close to one quarter of the average yearly salary in Japan.[2] This is a slightly lower figure compared to recent years, a decline which can be attributed to the influence of Covid-related restrictions on public gatherings. Funerals that only involve close relatives (家族葬 *kazokusō*) (Section 7.1.3) have also risen in popularity in recent years and are generally less expensive. The cost of funerals varies significantly according to their elaborateness, the number of attendees, the funeral company, and the region. The high cost of funerals in Japan, to both organizers and attendees, is a key reason driving the trend toward smaller ceremonies.

8.1.1 Ceremony Expenses

The calculation of the average funeral cost only includes ceremony expenses, which are paid directly to the funeral company. These costs include professional fees for body transportation and preparation; ceremony hall hire; the coffin, flowers, incense, and memorial photo; professional staff salaries; the cremation; and the urn and mortuary tablet. These are generally set by the funeral company and presented to customers in different packages at different price points. For example, one funeral home[3] in Tokyo advertises funeral packages including ¥330,000 for a cremation without ceremony, ¥550,000 for a simple family funeral without a flower altar, ¥825,000 for a family funeral with a flower altar, and ¥935,000, ¥1,100,000 or ¥1,650,000

DOI: 10.4324/9781003451914-8

for larger funerals each with more elaborate flower altars, coffins, and hearses. All packages include the basic services related to body preparation (coffin, mortuary tablet, dry ice, paperwork) and the ceremony (flower altar, hearse, staff, ritual tools, flower bouquet, memorial portrait). There are also optional extras and the ability to upgrade certain elements of the service. Funeral homes generally advertise the total price and the inclusions/exclusions for each package online. Funeral comparison websites, such as いい葬儀 (www.e-sogi.com), are very popular, and rank funeral companies by consumer reviews, star ratings, and estimated cost. Comparison website also commonly provide photographs of the ceremony hall and hearse.

8.1.2 Catering Expenses

In addition to ceremony costs, there are also expenses for catering, which are not part of the calculation of the average funeral cost in Japan. Most funeral companies work with restaurants to offer catering packages. These expenses include meals at the wake, funeral service, cremation, and interment, as well as gifts of gourmet food sent to attendees in acknowledgement of condolence payments. For example, families might send attendees cannisters of tea or boxes of biscuits (approximately ¥2,000 per person) or gourmet chocolates, dried seaweed, and olive oil (approximately ¥5,000 per person).

8.1.3 Religious Services Expenses

The funeral organiser must additionally pay for religious services. These fees are paid to religious officials, usually Buddhist priests, for their ritual performance, transportation, and accommodation costs. According to the Japan Consumer Association,[4] the average cost for religious services in 2020 was ¥425,000, up from ¥370,000 in 2017–2019.

This payment is known as *ofuse* (お布施), and it is generally paid directly to the priest on the day of the service, by placing cash into a white envelope. As this payment is often described by religious officials as a donation or expression of religious feeling, there are no set costs advertised by temples. This creates substantial uncertainty for families. In May 2010, when funeral company AEON (a subsidiary of the AEON retail conglomerate) published guidelines on *ofuse* amounts on their website, the Japan Buddhist Federation made an official request for the company to stop intervening in religious matters.

Associated with the category of religious services, most families also purchase a posthumous Buddhist name, or *kaimyō* (戒名), for the dead. While it is unusual for people to be ordained or take Buddhist precepts during their lifetime, most schools of Japanese Buddhism award people a precept name upon their death. This name is inscribed on the mortuary tablet and grave. There are examples of lay people being awarded *kaimyō* since the Kamakura Period (1185–1333), with the practice becoming popular in the 1600s.[5]

Kaimyō are divided into several ranks, considering factors such as Buddhist school, the deceased's social rank, age, gender, socio-economic status, and their piety or devotion. The name may reflect the personality traits of the deceased and incorporate characters from their relative's *kaimyō*. A standard *kaimyō* is six characters long. More expensive names are longer, personalized, and contain characters that indicate high status. Most people's *kaimyō* are not reported publicly. As an example, the *kaimyō* of the famous Japanese film director, Kurosawa Akira is「映明院殿紘国慈愛大居士」. It contains characters that reference his patronage of film and art, his broad mind, and affection the wide world. The *kaimyō* of Prime Minister Abe Shinzo is「紫雲院殿政響清浄晋寿大居士」. It contains characters that reference famous Buddhist monastics, political praise, purity, and eternal life. Both are bestowed with the highest rank of 大居士 in recognition of their contributions to public life.

Lower ranking *kaimyō* may cost ¥10,000 to ¥50,000, while higher ranking *kaimyō* may exceed ¥1 million. There has been severe criticism of Buddhist temples for this system, with accusations of price-gouging. Because they index socio-economic status and social rank, *kaimyō* have also functioned as a significant site of discrimination in the past.[6]

8.2 Interment Costs

The average funeral cost does not include expenses related to the interment of remains in a grave. Nationwide, the average combined cost of erecting a new conventional grave is estimated to be ¥1.524 million, a tree burial grave is ¥669,000, and a columbarium ¥776,000.[7] These costs can be broken down into three categories. First, the right of interment (永代使用料 *eitai shiyōryō*) must be paid upfront to the cemetery to secure use of the gravesite exclusively. Secondly, cemetery management fees (管理費 *kanrihi*) are paid annually to the cemetery for maintenance of the gravesite. Finally, gravestone fees (墓石代 *bosekidai*) are paid to erect the memorial. Once the grave is purchase and erected, it is possible for families to open the grave and inter remains themselves, however this process is usually completed by a professional and accompanied by ceremony, which incurs additional fees. Detailed description of the challenges of purchasing a grave in Japan can be found in Chapter 10.

8.3 Paying for Funerals

Before the professionalisation of funeral services in Japan, community cooperatives, known as *kumi* (組) or *kōgumi*, came together to assist with paying for weddings, funerals, festivals, and other communal projects (like planting rice or building houses). In this system, funeral and burial costs were distributed amongst multiple households. In contemporary Japan, the legally designated next-of-kin is usually responsible for funeral and disposition expenses (see Chapter 4). In general, funeral expenses must be paid in a lump sum to the funeral company (and other providers) within the period of one week to ten days after the funeral. If the responsible party is unable to pay in total they may choose to take out a 'funeral loan' (葬儀ローン) to pay in instalments. Funeral loans are offered by banks, credit unions, and by larger funeral companies directly.

8.3.1 Condolence Payments

Japan has a strong system of reciprocal gift giving. One way in which families recoup the cost of funerals is through the system of condolence payments or *kōden* (香典). These are cash gifts made directly to the family, on the day of the funeral or wake. Close intimates who are unable to attend may also send *kōden* in their place. The direct translation of *kōden* is "incense money" and is used for Buddhist ceremonies; other terms are used for ceremonies conducted in other religious traditions. Upon hearing of a death, the practice of sending incense as an additional mourning gift is also common, and indeed, grew in popularity during Covid-19, in light of restrictions on attending wakes and funerals.

The expected amount of *kōden* is dependent on one's degree of familiarity and relationship to the deceased or the bereaved, as well as one's age. For example, someone in their 20s may offer ¥5,000 at a friend's funeral, whereas an aunt in their 50s may offer ¥30,000 at their niece or nephew's funeral.[8] Married couples typically offer a joint *kōden*. Funeral company websites give advice on the typical or expected ranges for *kōden* for different degrees of relation or age. According to one survey (n = 1293) conducted by a funeral company in 2019, the average funds recuperated through *kōden* is ¥470,064 for one-day funerals, ¥1,239,457 for conventional funerals, ¥447,093 for family funerals and ¥150,455 for direct funerals.[9] The *kōden* is presented in cash, enclosed in a white envelope, inscribed with one's name on the front and the exact amount on the back. By custom, new bills are not used for *kōden*, and gifts in denominations of four or nine (homophones for 'death' and 'suffering') are considered taboo. In recognition of *kōden* payments, the family sends appreciation cards (礼状 *reijō*) and a small gift (香典返し *kōden-gaeshi*). The gifts are typically consumable items like sweets (Section 8.1.2).

In the economic depression of the post-war period, on the grounds that *kōden* and *kōden-gaeshi* imposed a major financial burden on families, a movement promoting the simplification of funerals and weddings, known as the 'New Lifestyle Movement' (新生活運動 *shin seikatsu undō*), spread. This movement is still influential in some communities in Japan today, where it is recommended to limit *kōden* to a small amount (like ¥1000) and to decline *kōden-gaeshi*.[10]

8.3.2 Insurance

Japan has a mixed system of public and private health insurance. When somebody enrolled in the public National Health Insurance or Medical Insurance for the Advanced Elderly schemes[11] dies, they are eligible to receive a one-time payment to assist with funeral expenses. This is known as the 'Funeral Benefit' or *sōsaihi* (葬祭費), and it is paid into the bank account of the person who organised the funeral. The payment is administered by the prefectural government where the death took place, and ranges from ¥30,000 to ¥70,000, depending on the locale. It is administered as a reimbursement and must be applied for by submitting a copy of the funeral bill within a period of two years. The payment is not subject to inheritance tax. The Funeral Benefit may not be paid if the chief mourner receives payment from the deceased's private health insurance fund; if a cremation-only rite or *chokusō* (rather than a full funeral) is held; or if the death was caused by a third party who is ordered to pay for the funeral as compensatory damages.

If the deceased held private health insurance, then they are instead eligible for a Private Funeral Benefit, called *maisōryō* or *maisōhi* (埋葬料・埋葬費). This is usually the case if the deceased was employed full-time for a private company or public office. Under Article 100 of the Health Insurance Law (1922) and its enforcement order,[12] the Private Funeral Benefit is uniformly ¥50,000, regardless of which health insurance society was used. However, some health insurance societies offer additional benefits. To receive the Private Funeral Benefit, the applicant must be in a dependent relationship with the deceased.

In addition to health insurance, Japan has the third largest life insurance market in the world, characterized by high market penetration and a large proportion of households covered by life insurance.[13] Various life insurance (生命保険 *seimei hoken*) and 'end-of-life' insurance (終身保険 *shūshin hoken*) products offer to pay benefits for funeral expenses and interment expenses.

8.3.3 *Mutual Funds*

Mutual Aid Associations or *Gojokai* (互助会) form the backbone of modern Japanese wedding and funeral services (see Section 6.3.2). The first Funeral and Wedding Mutual Aid Cooperative was founded in 1948 in Yokosuka by Funeral Director Nishimura Kumahiko.[14] Nishimura observed the difficulties families faced, in the midst of the post-war depression, to gather together large lump sums to pay for ceremonies. This was particularly the case for neo-urban families, who could not rely on the village community to raise funds. Mutual aid associations allow members to pay a monthly deposit toward a ceremony over a number of years. Typically, members are able to access the total cost of the ceremony within 6 months of joining, after which they can continue to gradually pay-off the remainder of the costs.[15] The mutual aid association may directly provide funeral services to members or delegate services to a subsidiary. For example, a scheme provided directly by the National Wedding and Funeral Mutual-Aid Association (全国冠婚葬祭互助会連盟), for metropolitan areas outside of Tokyo, consists of 100 payments of ¥10,000.[16] It includes hearse transportation and dry ice, the coffin, ceremonial clothes for

the deceased, memorial photograph, mortuary tablet, funeral at a ceremonial hall, and all associated meetings (including introductions to
Buddhist or Shinto priests). However, it excludes components like
offerings, incense, flowers, and alcohol for the wake. The mutual aid
system has had a significant impact on establishing Japanese funeral
companies as 'full service' operations, that comprehensively coord-
inate body disposal, funeral rituals, and memorials, where previously
they operated as vendors for funeral goods[17] (Section 6.1). They have
also led to the standardisation of service packages and fees across the
country.

8.3.4 *National Funeral Assistance*

For those facing extreme hardship, Japan has a National Funeral
Assistance (葬祭扶助 sōsaifujo) scheme, as established in Article
18 of the Public Assistance Act (1950). This payment is available to
established welfare recipients who are unable to pay for the funeral
of a deceased relative due to poverty. Welfare recipients who already
receive or received other public assistance are likely (but not guaranteed) to be approved for funeral assistance. If applicants have relatives
who are able to pay for the funeral, local authorities may require them
to do so. The scheme also applies when a welfare recipient themselves dies, and the cremation and funeral is conducted by an unrelated third party, such as a landlord or welfare officer. If the third
party can conduct the funeral with the assets left by the deceased, then
funeral assistance is not granted. A shortfall payment might also be
paid. Funeral assistance must be applied for before the funeral takes
place. The state pays three-quarters of the funeral assistance, and the
municipality pays one-quarter. However, according to Article 9 of
the Graveyard and Burial Act, where no third party is available, the
prefectural government is solely responsible for organizing the final
disposition and funeral. This payment is secured via application to
the prefectural office of the deceased's last address. The maximum
Funeral Assistance Payment is ¥200,000 for an adult and ¥165,000 for
a child respectively. As the number of elderly people receiving public
assistance has increased, so too has the number funeral assistance
payments. In Tokyo alone, 526 households received funeral assistance
in the 2008-09 financial year , but by 2022-23 this increased to 776.[18]

Notes

1 Japan Consumer Association 日本消費者協会,*第12回「葬儀についてのアンケート調査」報告書*, March 2023.

2 According to the National Tax Agency, the average yearly salary per salaried worker in 2022 was 4.61 million yen.
National Tax Agency 国税庁, 令和4年分　民間給与実態統計調査, accessed January 24, 2024, www.nta.go.jp/publication/statistics/kokuzeicho/minkan/gaiyou/2022.htm.

3 *Sōgi no uhara*, accessed February 27, 2024, www.souginouhara.com/plan/.

4 Japan Consumer Association 日本消費者協会,第12回「葬儀についてのアンケート調査」報告書.

5 Stephen G. Covell, "The Price of Naming the Dead," in *Death and the Afterlife in Japanese Buddhism*, ed. Jacqueline I. Stone and Mariko N. Walter (Honolulu: University of Hawaii Press, 2009), 298.

6 Fujii Masao 藤井正雄, 戒名のはなし (東京: 吉川弘文館, 2006).

7 Kamakura Shinsho 鎌倉新書, "第14回　お墓の消費者全国実態調査（2023年）霊園・墓地・墓石選びの最新動向," accessed December 20, 2023, https://guide.e-ohaka.com/research/survey_2023/.

8 Hikaru Suzuki, *The Price of Death: The Funeral Industry in Contemporary Japan* (Stanford: Stanford University Press, 2000), 85

9 Anshin Sōgi 安心葬儀, *(2019年調査) 香典の合計受取金額の平均・相場のデータ*, 2019, https://ansinsougi.jp/p-216

10 For example, see campaigns by Ashikaga City and Takasaki City.

11 国民健康保険 *kokumin kenkō hoken* or 高齢者医療制度 *kōreisha iryō seido*.

12 健康保険法 *Kenkō hoken hō* and 健康保険法施行令 *Kenkō hoken hō shikō rei*.

13 Statista, "Life insurance industry in Japan - statistics & facts," December 19, 2023, www.statista.com/topics/8996/life-insurance-industry-in-japan/#topicOverview.

14 Suzuki, *The Price of Death*, 54.

15 Tamagawa Takako 玉川貴子, 葬儀業界の戦後史 (東京: 青弓社, 2018).

16 Nihon Gojokai 日本互助会, "コースのご案内," accessed November 9, 2023, www.gojyokai.co.jp/course/index.html.

17 Suzuki, *The Price of Death*, 55; Theodore C. Bestor, *Neighborhood Tokyo* (Stanford: Stanford University Press, 1989), 199.

18 Bureau of Social Welfare, Tokyo Metropolitan Government 東京都福祉局, 令和4年度 福祉・衛生・統計年報, 107, accessed March 2, 2024, www.fukushi.metro.tokyo.lg.jp/kiban/chosa_tokei/nenpou/2022.html.

9   Cremation and Crematoria

9.1 Japan's Cremation Infrastructure

Cremation has had a mixed history in Japan, in some time periods promoted by the imperial household, Buddhist priests, and the government, and at other times entirely outlawed. For a detailed history of the emergence of cremation in Japan, see Chapter 2. In contemporary Japan, over 99.97% of the deceased are cremated.[1]

9.1.1   Crematoria Numbers, Management, and Capacity

As of November 2018, there are an estimated 1,454 crematoria operating in Japan. This figure decreased from 1,921 facilities in 1988 due to the decommissioning of ageing facilities and consolidation of small-scale operations.[2] Across these facilities, there are an estimated 5,320 cremation furnaces in operation, although exact estimates are difficult to confirm, given the long history and varied management of crematorium facilities. The vast majority of crematoria are operated by the cleaning and sanitation departments of municipal governments and are operated on a not-for-profit basis. As of 2018, according to a survey by the Japan Society of Environmental Crematory, there are 1,407 (of a total 1,454) of these public crematoria nationwide.[3] The number of crematoria owned and operated by private companies has increased in recent years and varies regionally.[4] For example, all but two crematoria in urban Tokyo are under private ownership.[5] In rural areas, particularly mountain hamlets, resident associations or community groups may operate these facilities, as they did traditionally, as there has been no transfer of these facilities to the municipality.

DOI: 10.4324/9781003451914-9

Japan's crematorium infrastructure faces notable problems of capacity. According to future population predictions by the National Institute of Population and Social Security Research, the number of annual deaths will exceed 1.5 million in 2030 and peak at 1.66 million in 2040[6] (see Chapter 3). This ageing population has placed a strain on crematoria capacity in recent years, particularly in Tokyo, where the wait for a cremation can be several days. The timing of cremation is extended by legal restrictions which stipulate that cremation (or burial) cannot occur within 24 hours of a death. Further, because cremation typically takes place as part of a larger ceremony, the average number of cremations processed by a single cremator each day is limited to around two.[7] This means that at many crematoria, the latest available cremation slot is between 2pm and 4pm. During natural disasters and mass death events, crematoria may operate overtime.

Additionally, cremation services less commonly take place on days that fall on *tomobiki* in the Japanese Auspicious Calendar. The Japanese Auspicious Calendar or *rokuyō* (六曜) is a six-day lunar calendar that ascribes differing conditions of fortune to each day.[8] Days marked as *tomobiki* (友引), literally 'pulling friends', are thought to be inauspicious for funerals and cremations, as the name implies that the living will be pulled by the dead toward the afterlife. In some regions, if a service is to take place on a "*tomobiki*" day then dolls are placed within the coffin as a substitute sacrifice for the living. While the auspicious calendar has less and less hold over Japanese daily life, it still impacts the scheduling of significant rites of passage. For example, one major Tokyo crematorium operates at 60% capacity on *tomobiki* days.[9]

Japan's cremation infrastructure also faces challenges. One estimate suggests that the cost of constructing a new crematorium has more than doubled, from ¥120 million in 1995 to ¥280 million in 2000.[10] Municipal governments generally do not receive subsidies from the national government to build new facilities. Since 1952, a low-interest loan system funded by the welfare pension insurance and the national pension fund under the jurisdiction of the Ministry of Health and Welfare has been applied to the construction of crematoria. The total estimated cost to the municipality of cremating a body (with facilities, maintenance, and depreciation included) was ¥30,000 in 1983 but nearly ¥50,000 in 1995. Crematoria tend to operate at a loss, and as government municipalities are legally responsible for the disposition of unclaimed remains, several municipalities offer free or heavily subsidized cremation services to residents. The average cost of a cremation in 1993 was ¥10,000.[11] In 2024, at a public facility, a cremation ranges from free to ¥50,000 for municipal residents, and at private facilities, from ¥70,000 to ¥80,000.

9.1.2 Cremation Process

In the early history of cremation in Japan, many permanent cremation grounds consisted of simple funeral pyres, sometimes contained under a roof. These were known as 'cremation sites' (焼場 *yakiba*). Some may additionally have had frames of stone or earthenware, positioned over a shallow trench in the ground. In the Edo period (1603–1867), cremation facilities known as *hiya* (火屋) began to emerge in major cities. As described in Chapter 2, Buddhist temples were deeply involved in the adoption and spread of cremation within Japan, and many early cremation grounds were located in temple precincts, known as 'cremation temples' (火葬寺 *kasōdera*).[12]

Mechanized cremators, consisting of an enclosed brick combustion chamber and chimney flue began to be built in the Meiji period (1868–1912)[13] following trends in Europe.[14] Some 19th-century designs for crematoria included the use of water as a filtration method to eliminate odours.[15] Crematoria of this period were built to accommodate the sitting coffins (座棺 *zakan*). Cremators for sleeping coffins (寝棺 *nekan*) emerged later. Early cremation pyres were fuelled largely by firewood, in a process that was likely both expensive and slow, taking nearly the whole day for a single cremation.[16] Alongside wood, heavy oil and coal were used as fuel sources in the early Taishō Era (1912–1926).[17] This period also saw significant advances in cremation technology via the introduction of electricity-powered cremators. In this system, an electric current is passed through nichrome wire in the walls and floor, creating enough heat to ignite coffins. By the early 1935, there were at least 50 electric crematoria operating across Japan.[18] They were praised for being cleaner and requiring less manual labour but were unreliable and could not be manually manipulated. Advances in cremation technology during this period were influenced by significant population growth in urban areas, as well as mass-death events, like the 1923 Great Kanto Earthquake. Kerosene and gas became the primary fuel sources for cremation in the 1960s and 70s, which significantly reduced exhaust fumes and led to greater combustion efficiency.[19] Heavy oil remains the fuel for a small number of Japanese crematoria alongside natural gas.

The introduction in the 1970s of afterburner or secondary burner technology, whereby unburned combustibles (soot and ash) are conveyed to an additional chamber for further incineration, made fumes more transparent and odour-free.[20] This technology also has the advantage of reducing compounds like ammonia and hydrogen sulphide, which contribute to exhaust odours.[21] Recently, prominent chimneys have become a rarer sight. As of 1995, only about 30% crematoria across Japan had visible smokestacks.[22] Recent technological advances in crematoria focus on particle collectors, filtration devices, and automation via computer control.[23] While crematorium facilities have become more and more advanced, older technology, including open air pyres, remained in use, for example, in Niigata and Hiroshima prefectures, well into the 1960s and 1970s.[24]

Two major types of cremation technology are used in Japan today, the "trolley" (台車式 *daisha-shiki*) and the "grate" (ロストル式 *rosutoru-shiki*). More than 97% of the crematoria built since the beginning of the Heisei period (1989–2019) use the trolley system, and they are slowly replacing grate system. At crematoria using the trolley system, coffins are placed atop a heat-resistant metal bench, which is moved into the incinerator chamber. Clay or cast-iron bricks at each corner of the chamber elevate the coffin from the floor. The machine cremates at 900 to 1,200 degrees centigrade and takes approximately 60 to 75 minutes. In the grate system, only the coffin is placed inside the cremator, on a metal grate which raises it above the bottom of the chamber by a few centimetres. This allows air to circulate underneath the coffin, thus increasing the rate and efficiency of combustion.[25] This grate system cremates at 800 to 950 degrees centigrade and takes approximately 35 to 60 minutes. A precursor to this system, 'Kimura-style cremation', which raises the coffin on rails, was patented in Japan in 1909.[26] Today, the grate system tends to be used in dense population centres where demand for cremation is high. A single cremator can be used to cremate up to five persons per day with this system (although such capacity is rarely utilised). However, these cremators can be more difficult to clean, as objects may get trapped in the grate, there are problems with odour, and bones are displaced. With the advent of the trolley system, an antechamber (前室 *maeshitsu*) was also added to the infrastructure of crematoria. Before this, coffins were moved directly into the incinerator in full view of families, creating distress.[27] Today, coffins are moved into an antechamber behind closed doors. The button that families press to close the doors to the antechamber is not directly connected to the doors of the cremator.

Functions including the ignition of the cremator, exhaust, and maintenance of temperature are largely automated processes at Japanese crematoria. However, some hands-on work is required. Crematoria workers monitor the progress of the cremation via the computer panel and via a small window in the back of the cremator. A long metal pole, known as a *derekki/dereki* (デレッキ/デレキ), is used to adjust the remains during the cremation, with the goal of retaining the bones in situ in their original position in the body.[28]

After cremation, the remains are allowed to cool in the antechamber for some 30 minutes. During this period, workers may rearrange the remains to ensure that key bone fragments are located in the correct position. They specifically look to identify the epistropheus bone, being the second cervical vertebra of the spine. This bone is known as the *nodobotoke* (喉仏), literally "throat buddha", because it resembles a buddha seated in meditation. When this bone survives the cremation process intact, it is interpreted as evidence that the deceased has travelled to the Pure Land. The *nodobotoke* is a highlight of the 'bone raising' ceremony (収骨/拾骨 *shūkotsu* or 骨上げ *kotsuage*) that commonly takes place at the crematorium with the bereaved family in attendance (Section 9.2). Cremulation, the process of milling bone fragments to produce ash, is rarely, if ever, performed. Instead, the remains are returned to families as a mixture of bone and ash. Private companies offering cremulation services have emerged in recent years in response to an increased desire for ash remains alongside the rising popularity of scattering.

9.1.3 Cremation Workforce

Contemporary crematoria, many of which additionally host ceremonies, hire a range of staff, including receptionists, caterers, and religious officiants, alongside cremator operators, or stokers (火夫 *kafu*). Stokers are responsible for introducing and removing remains from the cremator, observing the incineration, adjusting the temperature and location of remains to ensure efficient cremation. They also prepare the cremated remains for the bone raising ceremony (Section 9.2), by removing any remnants from the incinerated coffin and ensuring that the most significant bones are identifiable in their original location in the body. Although there exist qualifications for crematoria operators issued by the Japan Society of Environmental Crematory,[29] no prerequisites are required to become a stoker. The average annual income for this occupation is three to four million yen.

Historically, crematoria workers have been associated with people of a lower caste within the Japanese feudal system. From the medieval period, certain professional groups, including undertakers, abattoir workers, tanners, and executioners, were associated with *kegare* or moral defilement. Monastics or other workers associated with Buddhist temples and responsible for collecting remains, burial, and cremation, were described as belonging to the caste *onbō* (隠亡). During the Edo period (1603–1867) these castes were formalized under the Tokugawa class system, which gave certain occupations the hereditary status of untouchability. Members of these groups faced severe discrimination as outcasts and were forced to live in separate villages. The feudal caste system was officially dissolved with the 1869 Meiji Reformation's 'Emancipation Edict' (*Kaihōrei* 解放令); however, social discrimination continued well into the 20th century. Today, the term *onbō* is considered derogatory and is not used.

9.1.4 Crematoria Design

Over their history, crematoria in Japan have become more and more integrated with other ritual service providers, becoming multi-use facilities. Mizue Funeral Home, established in Tokyo in 1937, was the first of its kind to be equipped with a viewing area, waiting room, and funeral hall, and surrounded by parkland. Several contemporaneous commentators noted that the facility appeared more like a coffee shop than a crematorium[30]. According to a survey conducted in 1974, the majority (55.8%) of crematoria in Japan were stand-alone, purpose-built facilities.[31] About one third had ceremonial halls attached and 15% had an ossuary attached. However, trends toward consolidation suggest that crematoria are more and more likely to be combined with other facilities. Unattended cremations are rare in Japan, such that crematoria are designed with spaces for mourners to participate in ceremonies, including the pre-cremator hall (炉前ホール) or farewell hall (告別ホール), and spaces for mourners to collect cremated remains, known as the bone collection room (収骨室/拾骨室). The pre-cremator hall is an open space with multiple sets of floor-to-ceiling automated doors leading to cremators.[32] Pre-cremator halls are often constructed and decorated with polished marble walls and floors. Small crematoria with a small number of cremators may hold the pre-cremation farewell in a private room. The bone collection room is a small room centred around the tray cremated remains. This is where the *shūkotsu* ceremony takes place. In addition, crematoria typically have a lobby and waiting rooms. The facility may also have halls for holding funeral services, including a room with a Buddhist altar, and banquet rooms. In the backstage area, there are facilities for staff. Some crematoria are equipped with communal baths that are used by workers after their shifts.

With the rise of direct funerals, people are becoming more and more creative in how they use crematorium facilities. In the context of Japan, a direct funeral refers to an arrangement in which the body of the deceased is transported by a funeral company directly from the hospital or place of death to the crematorium without it being taken to a funeral hall for a service.[33] The body is then stored in a cold room at the crematorium facility.[34] Prior to cremation, only close family members or associates visit to bid farewell to the deceased, and there is typically no wake or funeral ceremony. The arrangement is preferable when there is a small number of mourners, and rental of a funeral hall is considered extravagant. Even at combined funeral and crematory facilities, mourners may hold a final send of for the deceased in a small meeting room adjacent to the mortuary, before moving to the crematory to witness the coffin entering the cremator.

9.2 Cremation Ceremony

Cremation can happen either before or after a funeral ceremony, although the latter is far more common. The timing is influenced by regional tradition, personal preference, and timing constraints. In areas where whole body burial was practiced until relatively recently, the funeral ceremony typically precedes cremation, while in areas where cremation was adopted earlier, cremation tends to precede the funeral.[35] After the funeral, the bereaved family and funeral company staff carry the coffin, load it into the hearse, and depart for the crematorium. Typically, the car that follows the hearse transports the chief mourner holding the mortuary tablet, the Buddhist priest, and another representative of the bereaved family holding a portrait of the deceased. Others follow in private cars. At the crematorium, the family submits a cremation application form and the Cremation Permit (火葬許可証 *kasōkyokasho*). The Cremation Permit is issued upon submission of the Death Notification Form (死亡届 *shibōtodoke*) to the local municipal government office (Chapter 3).

It is common for a short ceremony to be held at the crematorium. The coffin is placed on a trolley in the cremator antechamber. An incense stand, mortuary tablet, funerary portrait are arranged before the coffin. If a Buddhist priest has accompanied the family to the crematorium, they may burn incense and chant sutras. The chief mourner, followed by bereaved family, relatives, and acquaintances then come forward to offer incense. The window of the coffin is opened to allow attendees to bid their final farewell. The chief mourner may be then invited to push the button that opens the doors to the cremator and sends the coffin through. During the one to two hours when the cremation takes place, attendees typically remain at the crematorium in a waiting room, where they may enjoy a light meal (Chapter 7).

After cremation, staff wait for the remains to cool and then clean up the bones, removing any ash produced by the burning of the coffin. Mourners are then typically invited to participate in the 'bone raising ceremony'.[36] Beginning with the chief mourner, two people use chopsticks to pick up pieces of bone and place them into the urn. The chopsticks are then passed to another pair of mourners, who repeat the process. The bones are picked up in order, starting at the feet and moving toward the skull, such that when placed in the urn, the remains are arranged upright. The final piece of bone to be picked up is the *nodobotoke* or bone buddha,[37] if it has survived cremation. The symbolic meanings of this ritual are deep and varied. The Japanese word for 'chopsticks' is a homophone of the word 'bridge'. One reading is thus that 'passing between chopsticks' implies 'passing the deceased safely across the Sanzu River', the Sanzu being a mythical river in Japanese Buddhist tradition across which the dead must traverse to reach the Pure Land.

Ensuring that this ritual runs smoothly is one of the most important aspects of working at the crematorium. Before the ceremony, staff typically explain the process and meaning of the rite to family. They will also occasionally check the size of larger bones in advance of the ceremony to ensure that they will fit in the urn. This avoids having to crush or break bone fragments during the ceremony. Sometimes the remains are presented as a whole on the trolley, while at other facilities, important bones are removed and presented to mourners on a small tray. Staff may also rearrange the skeleton to ensure all bones are in the correct place, before inviting family to participate, and point out important fragments like the jawbone and humeri. There is distinct regional variation in this practice. In Eastern Honshū (the region encompassing Tokyo), the entire quantity of cremains is usually collected. In Western Honshū (the region encompassing Osaka and Kyoto), families usually only retain a small portion of bones, taken from the feet, knees, hips, sternum, and Buddha bone, and leave the rest of the remains at the crematorium.[38]

Tiny bone fragments and ash, too small to be handled with chopsticks, are known as "residual bone ash" or *zankotsubai* (残骨灰). This material may be collected up and poured into the urn or left at the crematorium. At some crematoria, residual bone ash is stored in aggregate and then periodically removed by specialized companies,[39] who send it to temples for ongoing storage and collective memorial. Some crematoria handle residual bone ash themselves.[40] Given these variations, the size of urns typically varies between different regions in Japan. Urns in Eastern Honshū are typically 25.5cm (height) × 21.7cm (width) with a capacity of 9,430 cubic centimetres, while urns in Western Honshū, where only partial remains are collected, are typically 20.5cm (height) × 18.2cm (width) with a capacity of 5,390 cubic centimetres. Smaller or larger urns may be used to accommodate different body sizes, or for the preservation of partial sets of remains. Urns are typically made out of white porcelain. The urn is placed inside a cedar wood box (骨箱 *kotsubako*) and is then wrapped in white silk brocade (骨覆 *kotsuōi*).

After the bone raising ceremony, mourners receive back the urn and the certified cremation permit, which serves as the permit for the future interment of the remains in a grave. By old custom, some mourners may choose to return home via a different route than the one they travelled to the crematorium, as a means to ward off the misfortune associated with death. At home, the urn is usually placed on a temporary altar alongside a mortuary tablet and a funerary portrait until the interment.

9.3 Cremated Remains

Conventionally, cremated remains are interred in an ancestral grave, alongside other members of the household. This usually occurs at or after the 49-day ceremony (Section 11.3.1), as part of a ritual known as *nōkotsushiki* (納骨式). It is common for a Buddhist priest to attend the cemetery with the family on this occasion and for there to be a short ceremony including chanting sutras, offering flowers, and burning incense. A range of alternatives to the ancestral grave are now available, including columbaria and tree burial, as described in Chapter 10. In different parts of Japan, cremated remains are poured from the urn into a muslin bag before being placed in the grave, or directly poured from the urn onto the earth floor of the grave vault, or the entire urn and its contents are interred.

The prospect of purchasing a new household grave has become more difficult, expensive, and burdensome in contemporary Japan (Chapter 10). Therefore, it is not uncommon for cremated remains to be stored in the home for months or years before interment. Typically, these remains are stored at or near a domestic Buddhist altar. Some cremated remains are also abandoned at crematoria. The incidence of unclaimed remains is rising, now representing 3.3% of all dead nationwide, and as a much higher proportion in some locations, such as Osaka, where it was 10% of all dead in 2015.[41] In previous eras, unclaimed remains generally belonged to unknown individuals, but today, unclaimed remains are generally the result of known next-of-kin refusing to accept responsibility for their disposal. At public crematoria, abandoned cremated remains become the responsibility of municipal staff. Many municipal crematoria have communal graves where ashes can be interred *en masse*. Given the separation of religion and state established in the post-war constitution, the municipality cannot perform (Buddhist) ceremonies to pacify the spirits of the abandoned dead. However, some municipalities hold non-religious memorial events, or ask voluntary social welfare associations to do so on their behalf.[42]

Scattering is not commonly practiced in Japan and the legal status of scattering on land is contentious (Section 4.2.2). In the past, organisations and individuals promoting ash scattering faced accusations of selfishness, a lack of filial piety, and Westernisation, although these critiques have tempered as the practice has increased in popularity.[43] There are a number of service providers offering scattering at offshore ocean locations accessible via boat. Before this can take place, cremated remains must be cremulated or pulverised. New services for bone pulverisation (粉骨 *funkotsu*), as well as washing, have emerged to meet this need. Unlike other locations in Europe and the United States of America, technological and environmental innovations regarding the disposal of human remains in Japan are generally focused on this treatment of cremated bones and ash. There has been little interest demonstrated in Japan in methods such as natural burial, human composting, or alkaline hydrolysis. Pulverisation is carried out mechanically, using a rotating mixer with ball-bearings, or by-hand, using a mortar and pestle. The result is remains of less mass and a more compact form. At some locations, the family may attend and take part in the pulverisation process. Bone washing services are typically employed when families wish to move the location of, or close down, an ancestral grave.

Ritual bone washing (洗骨 *senkotsu*) is also an established custom in other parts of Southern Japan, most notably Okinawa and parts of Kagoshima (Amami), which are home to cultural practices and peoples distinct to the rest of the mainland.[44] Traditionally in this custom, buried (not cremated) remains are disinterred and then hand washed by women on the occasion of the (re)opening of a grave for the newly dead, or when the remains reach the point of skeletonisation. However, this ritual placed a large emotional and practice burden on women, and after cremation became fully established in these areas from the 1970s, it was rarely practiced. This ritual is unrelated to the washing of cremated remains that is practiced in mainland Japan today.

Notes

1 The Ministry of Health, Labour and Welfare (MHLW) 厚生労働省, "Report on Public Health Administration and Services FY2021," accessed December 20, 2023, www.e-stat.go.jp/stat-search/files?page=1&toukei= 00450027&tstat=000001031469.
2 Japan Society of Environmental Crematory 特定非営利活動法人日本環境斎苑協会. 全国の火葬場数など, 2018, accessed December 20, 2023, www.j-sec.jp/files/f_1546821957.pdf, 1.
   The term "crematorium" here refers to facilities with three elements: furnaces, exhaust stacks, and buildings. Therefore, these statistics do not include outdoor cremation sites. Additionally, the society have their own survey methods, so the figures may differ from the Report on Public Health Administration and Services by the MHLW.
3 Ibid.
4 Yagisawa   Sōichi   八木澤壮一, "火葬場研究の目的と施設の概要: 火葬場の建築計画に関する研究I," 日本建築学会論文情報集 295 (September 1980), 96.

5 Kasō Kenkyu Kyōkai 火葬研究協会, 火葬場の立地 (東京: 日本経済評論社, 2004), 122.

6 National Institute of Population and Social Security Research 国立社会保障・人口問題研究所, "日本の将来推計人口," *Population Research Series* 347 (August 31, 2023), 9.

7 Yokota Mutsumi 横田睦, お骨のゆくえ: 火葬大国ニッポンの技術 (東京: 平凡社, 2000), 88.

8 The origins of *Rokuyō* can be traced to its transmission from China in the Kamakura period (1185–1333).
National Diet Library Japan 国立国会図書館, "六曜," 日本の暦, accessed November 29, 2023, www.ndl.go.jp/koyomi/chapter3/s3.html.

9 Kotani Midori 小谷みどり "火葬場が足りない？ 「数日待ち」のからくりとは……," 朝日デジタル, May 15, 2019, www.asahi.com/relife/article/12355405.

10 Yokota 横田, お骨のゆくえ, 84.

11 Ibid.

12 Asaka Katsusuke 浅香勝輔 and Yagisawa Sōichi 八木澤壮一, 火葬場 (東京: 大明堂, 1983), 86; Kawashima Reika 川嶋麗華, ノヤキの伝承と変遷 (東京: 岩田書院, 2022), 173–80.

13 Architectural Institute of Japan 日本建築学会, ed., 弔ふ建築: 終の空間としての火葬場 (東京: 鹿島出版会, 2009), 211.

14 Yokota 横田, お骨のゆくえ, 62.

15 Architectural Institute of Japan 日本建築学会, 弔ふ建築, 212.

16 Yokota 横田, お骨のゆくえ, 61.

17 Architectural Institute of Japan 日本建築学会, 弔ふ建築, 215.

18 Ibid, 217.

19 Ibid, 220. While gas is more efficient, there are concerns about gas supply to crematoria in the context of frequent natural disasters, particularly earthquakes, in Japan.

20 Ibid, 210.

21 Yagisawa 八木澤, 火葬場研究, 73.

22 Ibid, 60.

23 Architectural Institute of Japan 日本建築学会, 弔ふ建築, 211.

24 Asaka 浅香 and Yagisawa 八木, 火葬場, 93.

25 東京博善, "火葬炉の温度はどれくらい？ 骨だけ残る理由や火葬炉の仕組みを解説！," ひとたび *Magazine*, September 21, 2023, www.tokyohakuzen.co.jp/media/330.

26 Architectural Institute of Japan 日本建築学会, 弔ふ建築, 214.

27 Yokota 横田, お骨のゆくえ, 80.

28 Geta Hanao 下駄華緒, 火葬場奇談 (東京: 竹書房, 2022), 16–7.

29 Japanese Cremation Technology Management Association 日本火葬技術管理士会, accessed January 24, 2024, http://kanrishikai.sakura.ne.jp/index.html.

30 Yagisawa 八木澤, 火葬場研究, 69.

31 Ibid, 98.
32 As noted, while the public may perceive that the door leads directly to the cremator, crematorium workers in fact manually move coffins to the cremator to begin the process.
33 直葬 *chokusō* or *jikisō*; 火葬のみ *kasōnomi* or 'cremation only'. This term emerged in the 2000s, although the practice of cremation without ceremony had previously existed, for example, at cremations for recipients of national funeral assistance. One major motivation for the rise in cremation only services is the rising cost of funerals. Himon'ya Hajime 碑文谷創, "直葬とは何か," 大法輪 81, no. 5 (2014): 110–1.
34 Takeda Itaru 武田至 and Yagisawa Sōichi 八木澤壮一, "直葬の増加と火葬場の役割の変化について," 日本建築学会大会学術講演梗概集 (August 2011): 103–4.
35 Sekizawa Mayumi 関沢まゆみ, "火葬化とその意味" 国立歴史民俗博物館研究報告 191 (2016): 91–136 .
36 This rite has different names, including *shūkotsu* (拾骨, 収骨), *kotsuhiroi* (骨拾い), or, more conversationally, *kotsu'age* (骨上げ).
37 In Japan, the raised part of the nape of the neck, the Adam's apple, is known as the 'buddha bone'. However, this is cartilage and does remain after cremation. Instead, the second cervical vertebra has a protrusion in the center from a mortar-shaped bone, as if there are two sets of hands protruding from it. This is called the 'budda bone' after cremation.
38 Fabienne Duteil-Ogata, "New technologies and new funeral practices in contemporary Japan," in *Asian Religions, Technology and Science,* ed. István Keul (London: Routledge, 2015), 65; Satsuki Kawano, ""Who will care for me when I am dead?" Ancestors, homeless spirits, and new afterlives in low-fertility Japan," *Journal of the German Institute for Japanese Studies Tokyo* 26, no. 1 (2014): 118.
39 For example, Japan Environment Management Association (www.jema2014.com/index.html) and Sizen Cycle (https://sizencycle.jp/about/)
40 Boen/ Saijō Jitsumu Kenkyūkai 墓園・斎場実務研究会, ed. *Q&A墓園・斎場管理・運営の実務* (東京: 新日本法規, 2006), 736.
41 Anne Allison, *Being Dead Otherwise* (Durham: Duke University Press, 2023), 157.
42 Yamada Shinya 山田真也, "引き取り手のない故人の葬送と助葬制度," 無縁社会の葬儀と墓, eds. Yamada Shinya 山田慎也 and Doi Hiroshi 土居浩 (東京: 吉川弘文館, 2022), 54.
43 Kawano, "Who will care for me when I am dead?," 85–86.
44 Sekizawa Mayumi 関沢まゆみ, ed. *民俗学が読み解く葬儀と墓の変化* (東京: 朝倉書店, 2017).

10   Cemeteries and Interment

10.1 Types of Cemeteries

According to the report from Ministry of Health, Labour and Welfare, the number of cemeteries and historic burial sites in Japan stood at 870, 705 at the end of the 2021 fiscal year.[1] This can be broken down by the operating body: 30,208 operated by local governments, 58,743 by religious corporations, 585 by public corporations, 708,893 by individuals, and 72,276 by others. These classifications are based on the legal principle that local public bodies such as municipal governments should act as cemetery operators, only to be replaced by religious or public corporations when circumstances necessitate. In other words, cemeteries are required to be permanent and non-profit organisations, as they are deemed to be essential public services. However, if government supply cannot meet demand, then religious and public corporations are permitted to operate cemeteries on a license basis, as they are usually considered non-profit organisations.

Before the modern administrative framework was established, burial grounds were built and used in diverse ways by various groups. In fact, data from the above report shows that cemeteries owned by individuals and others – which can no longer be established under current law – are by far the most common. There exist numerous small burial sites that have been in use before the establishment of modern administration and are still maintained by families, clans, and villages. Furthermore, there are many examples of cemeteries that are managed by a religious organisation in name only and run by a corporation. As such, the actual administration of Japanese cemeteries is far more complex than legal classifications would suggest.

DOI: 10.4324/9781003451914-10

There has been a shift in the language used to describe cemeteries in Japan. *Bochi* (墓地) is the traditional term, but today *reien* (霊園, literally 'spirit parks') is far more common, a shift that broadly mirrors the distinction in English between graveyards or 'churchyards' and modern cemeteries or 'memorial parks'. The Tokyo Metropolitan Government changed the name of all metropolitan cemeteries from *bochi* to *reien* with the opening of Yahashira Cemetery in 1935.[2] This was motivated by a desire to dispel the gloomy image of traditional graveyards and to associate them with the bright and pleasant image of a park. In recent years, many private cemeteries in Japan have been given names such as 'Memorial Garden' or 'Memorial Park' to associate them with Western gardens. These facilities tend to have more natural landscaping and are often located in the suburbs.

10.1.1 Municipal cemeteries

Municipal cemeteries are operated by local authorities. They are characterised by low fees and indiscriminate acceptance of remains from people of all Buddhist schools and religions (including those of none). In many cases municipal cemeteries are established in the suburbs and take the form of parks, such that they also provide green space for local residents. Those who wish to establish a new grave in a municipal cemetery must meet certain requirements, such as being a resident and being the "Organizer of the Rituals".[3] Because the current supply of plots cannot meet the demand from citizens, an open lottery system is often used when applying for interment in a public cemetery. As such people cannot always acquire a grave in the cemetery of their choice. In 2023, across Tokyo metropolitan cemeteries, more than 8,000 applications were received for the just 210 available plots. Such supply issues vary regionally, but in general, people must win over tough competition to secure a grave in a municipal cemetery.[4]

In addition to municipal cemeteries established by local governments, publicly administered cemeteries include historic graveyards that have been used by village residents since the 17th century. These sites, called *"hikitsugi-bochi"* (引き継ぎ墓地), were transferred to local authorities from the late 19th century onwards. They are nominally owned by local authorities but remain managed and used by local residents. For example, in Osaka City, as of March 2023, of the 64 cemeteries owned by local authorities, only 10 are

Figure 10.1 Yagoto cemetery, a municipal cemetery in Nagoya. Photograph
   by Aki Miyazawa (author) on 26th October 2023.

directly maintained and managed by the city, and the rest are operated
by voluntary groups, usually consisting of current users.[5]

10.1.2   Temple Graveyards

Temple graveyards are managed by Buddhist temples. These
graveyards include not only those located directly within or adjacent
to the temple precinct, but also remote facilities. The links between
Buddhist temples and graveyards are historic, established well before
the modern cemetery administrative framework. Under the temple
certification system of the 17th century (Chapter 2), which designated
Buddhist temples with the sole responsibility for performing funeral
and memorial rituals, the number of temple graveyards increased
rapidly, as did the custom of erecting household graves.[6] The most
significant feature of temple graveyards is that those who wish to purchase a new grave must be parishioners. This trend continues despite
the end of the temple certification system and decreasing parishioner

numbers. Individuals seeking to establish a grave at a temple grave-yard might be charged parishioner joining fees alongside fees for the interment right.

Temple graveyards are generally interpreted as places necessary for religious activities (or 'religious property' under the Religious Corporation Law). Ceremonies in accordance with the particular teachings of the Buddhist school are usually conducted at the time of the interment. However, the religious beliefs of the subsequent inheritors of a family grave may change, sometimes leading to con-flict. People who have left the religion of the temple where their family grave is located may find themselves rejected for new interments by the temple because of their new faith or lack of faith.[7]

Urban temples are generally located in accessible locations, making them a popular place for establishing a grave. However, this also means that their available land is limited, and it is common to see large numbers of gravestones closely arranged on small plots of land in temple precincts. These restrictions have led to the consolidation of graves in urban temples, including the downsizing of graves, the con-struction of columbaria, and the creation of tree burial sites.

Figure 10.2 A temple graveyard in an urban area (Hōsenji Buddhist Temple, Tokyo). Image reproduced with permission from Hōsenji.

10.1.3 Enterprise/Private Cemeteries

Although there is no strict definition of the term 'enterprise cemetery' (事業型墓地 *jigyō-gata bochi*), it is often used to designate cemeteries managed by religious organisations that accept interments regardless of the religion of the deceased and/or bereaved. In Tokyo, it is reported that there are about 150 enterprise cemeteries.[8] In addition to large-scale park-like cemeteries built in the suburbs, there are also small-to medium-sized cemeteries in cities. There are also indoor cemeteries with graves arranged in enclosed rooms. Compared to municipal cemeteries and temple graveyards, enterprise cemeteries are characterised by less exclusionary practices, making them more accessible to people of a wider range of backgrounds as long as they have sufficient funds.

The establishment of new cemeteries by religious or public organisations runs contrary to the principle, set out in the Meiji era, that all new cemeteries should be governed by local authorities. However, after WW II, conditions for the establishment of new cemeteries were greatly relaxed in response to a lack of burial space. Since that period, religious and public corporations have been allowed to establish new cemeteries if it was difficult or impossible for public bodies (as set out in 'Regarding the Establishment of New Cemeteries' [1946]). From the 1970s onwards, a number of cemeteries have been developed in metropolitan areas by religious and other organisations and have begun to take over the majority of the supply of interment spaces. However, significant funding is required to develop large cemeteries and the complicated administrative procedures involved in establishing a new site make it practically impossible for a religious organisation to manage them alone. As such, it has become common for religious organisations to form cooperative relationships with private commercial companies to operate cemeteries.

Cemeteries established in this manner are subject to criticism. A frequent problem is the prevalence of so-called "name lending", in which commercial real estate agents or stonemasons "borrow the name" of an existing religious organisation, and essentially build and manage the cemetery independently. This arrangement is often unclear to the public. There have been cases, for example, of a for-profit company taking control of management and receiving most or all of the profits while placing final legal responsibility on the temple that is lending their name. This arrangement can destabilise the ongoing operation of the cemetery.[9] It has been reported that local authorities granting cemetery licenses often do so without conducting sufficient investigation into whether stable and sustainable operations are possible, partly because of the chronic shortage of cemeteries.[10]

10.1.4 Other Sites

There are many other sites for the interment of human remains that do not easily fit into the above categories. For example, there are a small number of private cemeteries and columbaria throughout the country run independently by Shinto shrines, Christian churches, and new religious organisations.[11] In addition, as mentioned earlier, there are many small burial sites that have been used by individual families and communities for a long time, since before the basic framework of cemetery administration was established. It is still common to see clusters of graves by the side of a road or in the corner of a field. In addition, there are special graves and cemeteries, such as military cemeteries dedicated to the memorialisation of conscripted soldiers, public ossuaries for victims of natural disaster and war, cemeteries set aside for foreigners who died during temporary residence in Japan,[12] and finally, mausoleums for the Imperial Family (Chapter 12).

10.2 Interment Practices

10.2.1 Purchase and Payment

When purchasing a conventional grave, three kinds of fees need to be paid: the cemetery fee, the headstone fee, and the cemetery maintenance fee.

The cemetery fee is the cost of purchasing a right of interment. It is paid only once when a plot in the cemetery is first contracted. The right is often described in vernacular as 'buying a grave' but is in fact a permit to inter remains and build memorials on a plot of land. Each cemetery stipulates the conditions by which the license may be revoked or resold. These conditions include, for example, five years of unpaid annual maintenance fees or no inheritor to succeed the grave. In Japan, this right of interment is often described as a 'perpetual right of use' (*eitai-shiyō-ken*), meaning that the cemetery can be used in perpetuity as long as the grave is maintained and managed by the user. Cemetery fees vary considerably depending on the area and the size of the plot. A typical fee ranges between ¥300,000 and 1 million yen, although some cemeteries in Tokyo, for example, Aoyama Cemetery, may charge more than 10 million yen for one plot.

In addition to the cemetery fees, customers must also pay to purchase and install the gravestone. There are various types of gravestones (Chapter 11), but most cost between 1 and 2 million yen, according to a survey conducted in 2022 by the National Association of Excellent Stonemasons (全国優良石材店 *Zenkoku-Yūryō-Sekizaiten*).[13] There is no specific time frame for erecting a gravestone after purchase. When a new grave is completed, a Buddhist priest may be invited to perform a religious ritual to imbue it with a spirit, and this rite can incur additional fees.

Cemetery fees and gravestone costs are only paid once, but regular management fees must also be paid. The management fee supports the maintenance of common areas of the cemetery, such as pathways, toilets, and green areas. According to a 2022 study by Kamakura Shinsho, the average annual management fee for a typical cemetery is approximately ¥8,000.[14] For some cemeteries, the ongoing payment of this maintenance fee is proof that the burial plot is maintained by the user.

10.2.2 Layout

There is no mention of cemetery design in national-level laws or enforcement regulations. This is because interment practices vary widely according to local tradition and custom, and the administration of cemeteries is designed to respect this variation. Hence, standards for the design of cemeteries and their buildings are regulated by the subsidiary rules of each local authority. For example, cemetery ordinance regulations in Yokohama, a large city to the West of Tokyo, set the following standards for cemetery layout[15]:

- The cemetery shall be located on land located a minimum horizontal distance of 110 metres from a school, park, or residential property to the boundary line of the cemetery, except where cremated remains are interred without gravestones, and where there are no public health hazards.

- The perimeter must be delineated by a fence or a hedge of densely planted trees.
- The land must have a proportion of green space, parking space, and road widths as specified in the Regulations.
- The cemetery should endeavour to establish a communal grave (refers to a grave where remains are excavated from a neglected grave and buried together)
- The area of each burial plot should not exceed 20 square metres.
- Gravestones or similar artefacts should be no more than 3 metres high.

Generally speaking, Japanese cemeteries do not segregate inter-ment areas by different ethnic groups, religions, or Buddhist schools. However, there are cases where temples or churches have purchased several plots in advance, effectively establishing their own area. In addition, as interment of cremated remains within family units is common practice, Japanese cemeteries do not generally have a sep-arate area for infant or children graves.

10.3 Types of Graves

10.3.1 Household Grave

The most typical form of grave in Japan is used by a single house-hold across multiple generations. The gravestone sits above a concrete vault dug into the earth, which contains space for the storage of mul-tiple sets of cremated remains. The gravestone is often marked with a family crest and engraved with the phrase 'grave of the XX family' or 'ancestral grave'. Chapter 11 gives detailed description of this grave design.

The conventional Japanese grave is premised on perpetual, multi-generational use by one household unit. It also becomes a symbol of that family line, whereby there is a normative cultural ideal that graves *should* be inherited and cared for by descendants. Graves in Japan are thus closely related to the flourishing of the household kinship system (家制度 *ie seido*). The household or *ie* (家) is the basic unit of Japanese social structure. The family name and respon-sibility for perpetuating the household are passed down through generations along the patrilineal line. It is common for the married heir to cohabit with their parents. These norms for the survival of the *ie* have had a significant impact on the culture, morality, and social structure of Japan.

This kinship structure is considered to have spread among the peasantry by the 17th century.[16] Under the Meiji regime of 1868, the *ie* was institutionalised in the Meiji Civil Code, which came into force in 1898.[17] This code also stipulated the succession of ancestral ritual property, including graves and Buddhist altars. Under this system, the head of the household is given great authority, including rights to the inheritance of ritual property (Article 987 of the Meiji Civil Code).[18] In other words, the grave is the symbol of the *ie* and the place for ancestral ritual, and the norm is that heirs of the *ie* must maintain and care for it for generations. After the first-born son, subsequent sons create new 'branch' households and establish a new grave, or, in the case of daughters, marry into a new household and enter the grave of their husband's *ie*.[19] The Meiji legislation also codified graves as the property and responsibility of the *ie* and not the community, government, or state.

This system was legally abolished with the introduction of the new Civil Code of 1947, as it was considered to be a remnant of the feudalistic nature of pre-war Japanese society. While no longer codified in law, the household has not completely disappeared from contemporary Japan.[20] For example, although the new Civil Code does not specify privileged succession by the head of the household, it stipulates that ritual property such as graves and Buddhist altars should be inherited by "the person who presides over rituals in accordance with custom" (Article 897), and where this sense of *ie* is still strong, this person is still more often than not the eldest son. These provisions in the new Civil Code also affect cemetery management rules. For example, the Tokyo Metropolitan Cemetery Ordinance of 1993 stipulates in Article 19 that the successor to the grave "must be the person who presides over the ancestral ritual". In other words, although the *ie* system has been abolished legally, the cultural norm that ancestral graves should be inherited and cared for by generations of patrilineal descendants remains strong.

Japan shifted from the household system to a nuclear family system in the post-war period, and as such, cultural norms and awareness of a household are slowly fading. Furthermore, Japan is now a 'super-ageing society' with a declining birth rate, such that there are fewer children to inherit and care for the grave. Without descendants, graves are vulnerable to be classified as 'neglected' and removed, in accordance with cemetery regulations (Section 4.2.3). Additionally, many people do not want to burden their children with the responsibility of a household grave, and so seek out alternatives. There has been growing demand for grave options that serve people who fall outside the patrilineal structure of the *ie*, including divorced and single people, people born out of wedlock, and LGBTIQ+ couples.[21] Since the 1990s, alternate grave systems that do not require succession by descendants have been proposed to replace household graves.[22] Some of the most prominent examples are introduced below.

10.3.2   *Communal Graves and Eternal Memorial Graves*

One solution to the problem of inheritance raised by the household grave system is graves that are managed and maintained by third parties. These grave types emerged in Japan in the 1990s and are increasingly popular. For example, communal graves (共同墓 *kyōdō-bo*), in which the remains of strangers are interred collectively, are now widely seen across Japan. Japan has a long tradition of communal graves in general. Those called *sō-baka* (総墓) are based on an established community such as a clan, village, temple, a local kinship group, or congregation, which manages and maintains the graves.[23] A new type of communal grave emerged in the 1990s, characterised by personal preference for communal interment, rather than blood relation or local community. Such graves were erected by temples, local authorities, private cemeteries, and even co-operative societies and nursing homes, and designed for people facing difficulties with bequeathing a grave.[24] Such graves have a variety of names in Japanese, including *gōsōsiki-kyōdō-bo, kyōdō-bo, gōsi-bo,* and *eitai-kuyō-bo*. Some are legally classified as columbarium due to their form in which several sets of remains are housed in a single facility.[25] Communal graves have several advantages, chiefly, that the long-term responsibility to care for the grave is secured within an organisation rather than the family. Further, the cost of interment is lower than the cost of constructing and maintaining a household grave.

The phrase *eitai kuyō bo* (永代供養墓) or 'eternal memorial grave' is often associated with communal graves. The term is mainly used by Buddhist temples and private cemeteries, due to the inclusion of the Buddhist term *kuyō*, which is not used in public cemeteries. The phrase suggests that the temple will permanently protect and give ritual care to each individual grave on behalf of the family. However, often the dead is only individually interred and venerated for a limited period of time, such as 13 years, before being transferred to being enshrined collectively with others. Further, despite the promise of permanency, the expression *eitai* only really applies as long as the temple or company remains in operation.[26]

10.3.3 Columbaria

Although the interment of remains in graves has long been in the norm in Japan, there is historical precedent for the use of columbaria. A turning point came in 1911, when columbaria were officially authorised as an alternative to graves, provided that they were fire-resistant and sufficiently protective of the remains.[27] In the current version of the Graves and Burial Act (1948) columbaria are listed as a facility for the storage of human remains alongside cemeteries. Until recently, columbaria were considered a temporary storage method used until a grave could be purchased,[28] but today, many people prefer to use columbaria due to aforementioned considerations of inheritance and affordability.[29]

Although there are several types of columbaria, including shelf-style, locker-style, and altar-style, they are all essentially indoor facilities with multiple niches dedicated to the storage of remains. These facilities are sheltered from the elements and often have air-conditioning, benches, and seats, to ease visitation. The niches (or 'shelves' or 'lockers') can also be easily customised with photographs, incense, and offerings like artificial flowers. The number of high-tech columbaria housed in multi-storey buildings in urban centres has particularly increased in recent years. So-called 'automatic-conveyance columbaria' are equipped with robotic delivery systems, IC card access, and other security measures. They first emerged in Tokyo in the 1990s and have subsequently spread through urban centres.[30] At these facilities, boxes of cremated remains are transported through the facility using mechanised arms and conveyor belts, travelling from backstage storage racks to individual visitation booths. The booths offer a space for families to visit remains, light incense, and offer prayers. But because they are shared, they cannot be easily customised with personal items, and indeed, offerings of flowers or sweets are banned. This system does, however, allow the columbarium to store many tens of thousands of sets of remains in a small building in the middle of the city, often located near other facilities and public transport.

Figure 10.3 A visitation booth at an automated conveyance columbaria in Tokyo. Photograph by Hannah Gould (author), 2021.

10.3.4 Tree Burial

Tree burial is a method of burying remains in the ground using trees and other plants as grave markers. Unlike 'natural burial' or 'green burial' in the West, in Japan, the term 'tree burial' exclusively refers to the interment of cremated remains, not whole body burial. In 1999, a Buddhist temple in a local city in Iwate Prefecture, in northern Japan, started this interment style with the goal of protecting the local mountains from development and enabling the regeneration of the natural environment by planting trees as grave markers and maintaining them as cemeteries.[31] One of the characteristics of tree burial is that no gravestone is erected, and the remains are placed directly in the earth rather than enclosed in a stone vault. As such, unlike family graves, there is no need to keep up maintenance from generation to generation. Because of this convenience, tree burial is now widely favoured by

Figure 10.4 Tree burial site (Sakurasō) of NPO Ending Center in Machida Izumi Jōen, Tokyo. Reproduced with Permission of the Ending Centre.

people who do not wish to leave a grave to their successors. However, there is no clear definition of the term tree burial and, partly because the temple that invented tree burial did not register any trademark, a great variety of tree burial styles can be found across Japan. The most common type is one in which a symbolic tree, such as a cherry blossom, is used as a communal grave marker and several remains are buried around it.[32] The interment spot may be marked with or without a plaque or other marker. There are also tree burial sites which initially inter remains around a tree individually, but after a certain period of time, exhume remains and reinter them collectively.

10.4 Reinterment and Grave Closure

Reinterment (改葬 *kaisō*) refers to the transfer of an interred corpse or cremated remains to another grave or columbarium. As with burial and cremation, it is necessary to obtain permission from the municipal authorities to perform a reinterment. The procedure and documents required to complete the application are stipulated in the enforcement regulations of the Graves and Burial Act. In Japan, reinterment is not uncommon, with around 120,000 reinterments taking place nationwide in 2021–2022 fiscal year.[33] In recent years, there has been a noticeable increase in remains being removed from household graves and placed into columbaria or communal graves. The household grave is then closed permanently, a process known as *haka-jimai* (墓じま い). Grave closure is often motivated by people's concern for a lack of household successors, itself a product of Japan's low birth rate and ageing population.

Grave closure can be expensive, with costs relating to the physical removal of remains and dismantling of the gravestones, administrative fees paid to the cemetery, and costs related to reinterment of remains in a new location. These costs vary widely depending on the cemetery but are estimated to range between ¥300,000 and ¥3,000,000.[34] If families are temple parishioners, then they may need to pay a significant fee for a closing memorial service and donation to the temple. Although it is also possible for a third party, for example, a cemetery administrator, to resell and reuse a grave, the procedure is more complicated. In the past, the applicant needed to confirm the absence of a relative willing to take on the management of a grave by advertising at least three times in two or more different daily newspapers. However, due to rising concerns regarding the increasing number of neglected graves, for which management fees cannot be collected and which put pressure on interment space, enforcement regulations were amended in 1999 to simplify reinterment procedures. The simplified procedures include posting a clearly visible notice on the neglected grave plot, and placing a public notice in an official gazette, requesting that the relevant party get in touch with the cemetery.

Although the criteria for neglected graves differ from municipality to municipality, according to a 2022 survey by the Ministry of Internal Affairs and Communications, 58.2% of the 765 municipalities with public cemeteries and columbarium reported that they have neglected graves in their facilities.[35] In the 2021 financial year, there were 3,309 cases of reburial of neglected graves nationwide, of which nearly 60% were carried out in populous urban areas such as Tokyo, Osaka, and Aichi.

In response to rising numbers of neglected or abandoned graves, various temples, cemeteries, and local governments have begun to establish resting places for unwanted gravestones, sometimes

Figure 10.5 A notification board placed on a family grave in Aoyama
        Cemetery, Tokyo. The image has been edited to obscure the
        family name. Photograph by Aki Miyazawa (author).

poetically labelled *ohaka no haka* (お墓の墓) or 'the grave of the
graves'. While many of the gravestones are disposed of by pulverising
the marble for reuse, the central stone engraved with the family name
may be preserved because it is thought to retain some trace of the
spirit of the dead. Cemeteries often have areas dedicated to displaying
mounds of these headstones, known as *muen-dzuka* (無縁塚), and may
give offerings or ask Buddhist priests to perform prayers before them.

10.5 Whole Body Burial

Despite the fact that whole body burial was very common throughout
Japan until the pre-war period, it is now extremely rare, as almost all
people in Japan are cremated. In cemeteries where burial was originally practiced, the transformation of graves from burial sites to interment sites is an ongoing process. The remains of those already buried

are exhumed, a grave with a vault is re-erected on the site, and the remains are reinterred. Although burial is not illegal in Japan, local government ordinances and regulations, as well as the rules set by each cemetery, mean that in practice, there are few places where burial is possible.

In this context, one recent issue is the provision of cemeteries for Muslims.[36] Immigrants, mainly from countries such as Pakistan, Indonesia, and Bangladesh, move to Japan for work or study, and some seek to settle permanently in Japan. Traditionally, Muslims who die in Japan have been repatriated and buried in their home country. However, partly due to the high costs involved in repatriation, there is a growing demand for burial sites in Japan. It is said that there are currently only 13 cemeteries which accept Muslim burials across the country.[37] However, due to people's aversion to burial itself and to broader cultural prejudices among local residents, the opening of Islamic cemeteries has faced many obstacles and there continues to be a shortage of burial space.[38]

Some municipal ordinances and regulations prohibit burial entirely, but many do not specify any prohibition and give details of the depth

Figure 10.6 One of the Japanese Muslim graveyards in Monjuin, Yamanashi Prefecture. Photograph by Aki Miyazawa (author), 1st October 2023, with permission from Monjuin.

of the grave plot or the minimum clearance between the coffin and ground level. Depth is specified as 1.5m, 2m, or 1.8m, while the clearance is often specified as 1m to 1.5m. Although there are no regulations regarding the material or construction of coffins under Japanese law, the size of commercial coffins is largely determined by the size of the cremation furnace (Chapter 9).

Notes

1 Ministry of Health, Labour and Welfare 厚生労働省 "Report on Public Health Administration and Services 2021FY," accessed December 20, 2023, www.e-stat.go.jp/stat-search/files?page=1&toukei=00450 027&tstat=000001031469.

2 Fujii Masao 藤井正雄, お墓のすべてがわかる本 (東京：プレジデント社, 1991), 143; Boen/ Saijō Jitsumu Kenkyūkai 墓園・斎場実務研究会, ed., *Q&A墓園・斎場管理・運営の実務* (東京: 新日本法規, 2006), 62.5.

3 The term "Organizer of the Ritual" (祭祀の主催者 *saishi no shusaisha*) is a legal designation that refers to the successor, who inherits and cares for the family grave and the Buddhist altar, according with Article 897 of the Civil Code. However, in consideration to the recent trend towards nuclear families and individualisation, the Tokyo Metropolitan Government additionally lists other person as eligible applicants for a new grave: those who acted as chief mourner at the funeral, those who acted as the host of the memorial service, those who acted as notifiers of death, and those who applied for cremation permission.
Tokyo Metropolitan Park Association 東京都公園協会, 令和5年度 都立霊園公募受付状況と抽選会について, accessed September 18, 2023, www.tokyo-park.or.jp/reien/use/new_user/pdf/reienR5_rule.pdf, 4.

4 Ibid.

5 Osaka City 大阪市, 市設霊園のご案内, accessed 19 September, 2023, www.city.osaka.lg.jp/kankyo/page/0000369336.html.

6 Mori Shigeru 森茂, 日本の葬送・墓地：法と慣習(京都：法律文化社, 2013), 143.

7 Mori Kenji 森謙二, 墓と葬送の現在 (東京: 東京堂出版, 2000).

8 Kawazoe Yoshiyuki 川添善行 and Kondō Mayuko 近藤真由子, "首都圏における事業型墓地開発の実態とその対策,"土地総合研究所, (2005), 12–5.

9 "抜け道墓地 被害続々," *Asahi Shinbun*, February 21, 2011.

10 MHLW 厚生労働省, 墓地経営・管理の指針等について, December 6, 2000, www.mhlw.go.jp/topics/0104/tp0413-2.html.

11 Kawamata Toshinori 川又俊則, "教会墓地にみるキリスト教受容の問題," 年報社会学論集 11 (1998): 191–202; Inoue Nobutaka 井上順

孝, Kōmoto Mitsugu 孝本貢, Tsushima Michihito 対馬路人, Nakamaki Hirochika 中牧弘允, Nishiyama Shigeru 西山茂, eds., 新宗教事典 本文篇 (東京： 弘文堂, 1994), 426–444; Fabienne Duteil-Ogata, "Emerging Burial Space and Rituals in Urban Japan," in *Invisible Population: The Place of the Dead in East Asian Megacities*, ed. Natacha Avelin-Dubach (London: Lexington Books, 2012), 50–71.

12 In Yokohama, there are four foreigner-specific cemeteries: Yokohama Foreign General Cemetery, the Chinese Cemetery (Chūka-Gisō), and Yokohama War Cemetery.

13 Zenkoku Yūryō Sekizaiten 全国優良石材店, 第35回（2022）全国統一全優石 お墓購入者アンケート調査結果発, accessed September 22, 2023, www.zenyuseki.or.jp/pr/details.html?id=231.
The Kamakura Shinsho's 2022 survey also showed that the average national price for a headstone was 1,106,000 yen.
Iiohaka いいお墓,【第13回】お墓の消費者全国実態調査（2022年）霊園・墓地・墓石選びの最新動向, accessed September 22, 2023, https://guide.e-ohaka.com/research/survey_2022/.

14 Ibid.

15 Yokohama City 横浜市, 横浜市墓地等の経営の許可等に関する条例, accessed November 1, 2023, https://cgi.city.yokohama.lg.jp/somu/reiki/reiki_honbun/g202RG00001692.html#e000000057;
横浜市墓地及び納骨堂に関する条例施行規則, accessed November 1, 2023, https://cgi.city.yokohama.lg.jp/somu/reiki/reiki_honbun/g202RG000000800.html#e000000061.

16 Yano Keiichi 矢野敬一, "家の歴史認識" in 現代家族のリアル：モデルなき時代の選択肢, eds. Nakagomi Mutsuko 中込睦子, Nakano Kiwa 中野紀和 and Nakano Yasushi 中野泰 (京都：ミネルヴァ書房, 2021), 273–92.

17 Yohko Tsuji, "Death policies in Japan," in *Family and Social Policy in Japan: Anthropological Approach*, ed. Roger Goodman (Cambridge: Cambridge University Press, 2002), 177–99.

18 It is stipulated that "ownership of genealogical records, ritual goods, and tombs belongs to the prerogative of patriarchal inheritance".

19 Satsuki Kawano, "Finding Common Ground: Family, Gender, and Burial in Contemporary Japan," in *Demographic Change and the Family in Japan's Aging Society*, eds. John W. Traphagan and John Knight (New York: State University of NY Press, 2003), 125–44.

20 Allison Alexy and Richard Ronald, eds., *Home and Family in Japan: Continuity and Transformation* (Abingdon: Taylor & Francis, 2011).

21 Anne Allison, *Being Dead Otherwise* (Durham: Duke, 2023), 40.

22 For more on this issue, see: Tsujii Atsuhiro 辻井敦大, 墓の建立と継承 ―「家」の解体と祭祀の永続性をめぐる社会学 (東京：晃洋書房, 2023).

23 Mori Kenji 森謙二, "総墓の諸形態と先祖祭祀," 国立歴史民俗博物館研究報告 41 (1992): 255–315.

24 Jieun Kim, "Necrosociality: isolated death and unclaimed remains in Japan," *Journal of the Royal Anthropological Institute* 22, no. 4 (2016): 843–863.

25 Tsujii 辻井, 墓の建立と継承.

26 Mori Kenji 森謙二, 墓と葬送の現在.

27 Yamada Shinya 山田慎也, "納骨堂の成立とその集合的性格," in 現代日本の葬送と墓制, eds. Suzuki Iwayumi 鈴木岩弓 and Mori Kenji 森謙二 (東京: 吉川弘文館, 2018), 63–86.

28 Fujii Masao 藤井正雄, 現代人の信仰構造 (東京: 評論社, 1974), 138.

29 Kamakura Shinsho 鎌倉新書, 【第14回】お墓の消費者全国実態調査 (2023年) 霊園・墓地・墓石選びの最新動向, accessed December 20, 2023, https://guide.e-ohaka.com/research/survey_2023/.

30 Daisuke Uriu, William Odom and Hannah Gould, 2018," Understanding Automatic Conveyor-belt Columbaria: Emerging Sites of Interactive Memorialization in Japan" in *DIS '18: Proceedings of the 2018 Designing Interactive Systems Conference*, 747–752.

31 Sébastien Penmellen Boret, *Japanese Tree Burial: Ecology, Kinship and the Culture of Death* (London: Routledge, 2014).

32 Cherry Blossoms are a rich symbol of Japanese culture, associated with impermanence and beauty, as they only bloom momentarily. Emiko Ohnuki-Tierney, *Kamikaze, Cherry Blossoms, and Nationalisms: The Militarization of Aesthetics in Japanese History* (Chicago: The University of Chicago Press, 2010).

33 MHLW 厚生労働省, "Report on Public Health Administration and Services 2021FY."

34 お仏壇のはせがわ,　お墓じまいの費用平均はいくら？総額と内訳、払えない場合の対応も解説, February 3, 2022, www.hasegawa.jp/blogs/ohaka/ohakajimai-price

35 Ministry of Internal Affairs and Communications Administrative Evaluation Bureau 総務省行政評価局,　墓地行政に関する調査—公営墓地における無縁墳墓を中心として— (2023), 10.

36 Shinji Kojima, "To Bury or Not to Bury: Muslim Migrants and the Politics of Funerary Rights in Contemporary Japan," *Japan Focus: The Asia-Pacific Journal* 21, no.11 (2023): 1–21.

37 For example, Hokkaido, Yamanashi, Ibaraki, Saitama, Shizuoka, and Kyoto have Muslim cemeteries or dedicated sections for Muslim burials in their cemeteries.

38 Suzuki Kantarō 鈴木貫太郎, ルポ 日本の土葬 (東京: 宗教問題, 2023).

11 Commemoration

Japanese death rituals extend beyond the immediate wake, funeral, and cremation to multiple years or generations. An elaborate retinue of material goods and ritual practices are used across this lengthy posthumous period. The relationship between the living and the dead during this period has been described as one of mutual obligation and reward, whereby the living care for the dead, and in return, the dead offer the living guidance and protection, as well as blessings of good fortune.[1] By making offerings, the living help the dead mature from unruly, immature spirits into buddhas and ancestors. When they are neglected or abandoned, the usually benevolent dead may become *muenbotoke* (無縁仏) or 'bondless buddhas' who wander the world as pitiful creatures, causing various misfortunes for the living.[2]

11.1 Kuyō

The term *kuyō* (供養) is used to refer broadly to offerings, rituals, and other material practices of care for the dead. The term derives from the Sanskrit term for *puja*, meaning offerings to the buddha and sangha, but almost exclusively refers to offerings made to the dead in contemporary Japan. At a minimum, this might describe placing incense, fruit, and flowers at a grave or altar dedicated to the deceased, but it can also extend to elaborate rituals with Buddhist priests chanting sutras. Further, *kuyō* has extended beyond its original Buddhist context, and is now performed at other religious organisations and by non-religious organisations and people. The Japanese culture of 'caring for' the dead has been described in other East Asian and Buddhist cultures, in contrast with Western cultures of 'memorialisation', in which the

DOI: 10.4324/9781003451914-11

dead are primarily remembered by the living.[3] In contemporary Japan, both practices of *kuyō* and memorialisation have been observed, often intermingled in the same rituals and commemorative materials.[4]

Kuyō is not only performed on the occasion of the death of an adult human. Since at least the Edo period (1603–1868), there has been a tradition of *kuyō* being performed for non-sentient beings, objects, animals, and foetuses. There are *kuyō* rites for domestic and professional tools, including needles, scissors, eyeglasses, and more recently, computers, *Tamagotchi*,[5] and the robot dog AIBO,[6] and in the category of animals, for whales,[7] animals used in scientific experiments,[8] and more recently, domestic pets, whom have come to be considered as part of the family.[9] The list of entities subject to *kuyō* has changed throughout history and displays significant regional variation and idiosyncrasies. During the second half of the twentieth century, Japan experienced a "*kuyō* boom" driven by rapid economic growth, which prompted professional organisations to sponsor rites for the tools of their trade as repayment for good fortune.[10] These included scissor rites sponsored by hairdressers and needle rites sponsored by seamstresses and tattoo artists.[11] *Mizuko kuyō* (水子供養) describes rituals performed for aborted, stillborn, and miscarried foetuses. The Bodhisattva Jizō, the guardian of children and wayward souls, is commonly evoked in these rituals. *Mizuko kuyō* rites are a relatively recent phenomenon, having risen to prominence in the 1990s.[12]

11.2 Material Objects (*Kuyōhin*)

The Japanese dead are considered to be multiply located in different sites and objects. Offerings to the dead are commonly made at the household grave (where the cremated remains are stored), at the domestic Buddhist altar (where the mortuary tablet is stored), and at Buddhist temples or other religious institutions. The dead are also commonly said to 'return home' from the mountains to the household during *Obon*, the festival of the ancestors (Section 11.3.2).

11.2.1 Graves

11.2.1.1 Inherited Household Graves

Traditional Japanese graves (Figure 11.1), which inter the remains of the household, are known as *iebaka* (家墓). Graves for individuals,

Figure 11.1 Photograph of an inherited household grave, Chiba Prefecture, 24th May 2016. Photograph by Aki Miyazawa (author).

couples, bilateral relations, or communities are less common, but available. Typical graves are made of grey or black polished marble slabs that fit together to delineate and protect the space of interments. The central part of the grave is the top headstone or *saoishi* (棹石), which is engraved with the family name and crest. This sits atop one or more stone slabs that cover a chamber excavated into the earth, known as the *karōto* (カロート), where the remains are interred. The size and style of the interment chamber depends on the region and cemetery. In cases where the cremated remains are removed from the urn and poured into the chamber directly, the bottom of the chamber is usually open to the earth. Where the cremated remains are interred in urns, the chamber is typically enclosed with stone.

   The most common Japanese grave design (和型墓石 *wagataboseki*) consists of a vertical pillar of stone for the headstone and is a simplified version of a Buddhist stupa. The headstone, sometimes known as the Buddha stone, sits atop three stone slabs, known as the heaven, human, and earth stones respectively. Additionally, a dais for offerings, two flower vases, a water container, and an incense brazier are positioned in front of the headstone. There are many different styles of *saoishi* or headstone, including flat top, rounded, prismatic, *ihai* style, and picture frame style. The conventional *wagataboseki* style of grave became popular during the Edo period (1603–1868). Before this, graves typically more closely resembled a Buddhist 'five ringed pagodas' (五輪塔 *gorintō*), which housed the relics of a saint or famous teacher. The five stones that make up the *gorintō* have different symbolism, each representing sky, wind, fire, water, and earth. Recently, 'modern' or 'Western'-style graves (洋型墓石 *yōgata boseki*), with horizontal headstones, have grown in popularity.

More elaborate graves contain additional marble structures and may be enclosed within a low stone fence. This may include a *boshi* (墓誌) or *reihyō* (霊標) stone, which lists the individual names of all those interred, as well as a lantern, water basin, individual gravestones for pets or *mizuko* and statues of Buddha. The surrounding area can be decorated with gravel or plants. New graves are typically designed by and purchased from stone masons. Private cemeteries may have designated stone mason companies or enforce restrictions on the type and size of memorial to ensure a uniform look. Upon deciding the grave design, a deposit is usually paid, and construction begins. It takes approximately 2 to 3 months for a grave to be constructed, at which time the full balance is due. Then, a consecration ritual (開眼 法要 *kaigen hōyō*) is held to sacralise the grave. This ritual is often combined with the first interment of remains and the 49th day, 100th day, or 1-year anniversary of the death. A Buddhist priest typically conducts the ceremony. The new headstone may be wrapped in a white cotton cloth, which is removed as part of this rite.

Once established, families, friends, and colleagues of the deceased may visit a grave to pay their respects as they feel, or on important occasions, such as an anniversary, the *Obon* festival, or equinox period. The practice of visiting a grave is known as *haka-mairi* (墓参り). A typical visit begins with washing the gravestone down with fresh water and clearing off any debris. The water bowl is filled with fresh water. The grave area is swept, and any ornamental plants are tended to. Offerings of food and flowers are placed in front of the grave and incense or candles are burned. In some cases, colleagues of the deceased may leave business cards at the grave to communicate to the family that they have visited.

In many Buddhist schools, it is common for major graveside services to be marked by the erection of carved wooden planks, known as *sotoba* (卒塔婆). *Sotoba* typically have five notches, mimicking the five-ringed stupa that stores Buddhist relics, and are inscribed with Sanskrit characters for the five elements. They cost between ¥3,000 and ¥5,000, paid directly to the temple. *Sotoba* are lined up behind the grave, and the offerings are considered an act of merit making for the deceased. Older or decayed *sotoba* may be cremated by temple staff.

In the place of traditional graves, in recent decades there has been a sharp rise in alternative interment options, such as columbaria, communal graves, and tree burial sites. These options are described in detail in Chapter 10.

11.2.2 Ihai *(Mortuary Tablet)*

Ihai (位牌)[13] are wooden tablets inscribed with the posthumous name of the deceased. More than records of the deceased, *ihai* are treated as "receptacles (依り代 *yorishiro*) or even duplicate bodies (分身 *bunshin*) for the spirits of the dead".[14] Indeed, a popular aphorism about *ihai* is that they are the first thing that people run to save when a fire breaks out.

Ihai have syncretic origins, blending Confucian, Buddhist, and folk traditions together into a single object. *Ihai* appear to have been introduced from China during the Song dynasty (960–1279), overlapping with the Japanese Kamakura period (1185–1333),[15] just as Buddhist and Confucian memorial practices were being syncretised. They were introduced to Japan via the Zen school of Buddhism. The term *ihai* literally means 'rank tablet' and is thought to derive from *shinshu* (神主), tablets inscribed with the official rank and name of the deceased in Confucian funeral rites in China. At the same time, *ihai* appear to also be influenced by Buddhist *sotoba* (wooden planks arranged behind a grave) and the votive tablets (霊代 *tamashiro*) placed on spirit shelves in Japanese folk religion, practiced before Buddhism's arrival.[16] The practice of making *ihai* spread to the wider populace during the Edo period (1603–1868). All schools of Japanese Buddhism direct their followers to make *ihai*, except for Pure Land Buddhism. In Pure Land Buddhism, an individual's Buddhist precept name, awarded to them during their lifetime, is instead written in an ancestral book or hanging scroll (法名軸 *hōmyōjiku*).

There are many different types of *ihai*. These include:

- *Uchi-ihai* (内位牌) or *kari-ihai* (仮位牌) are temporary tablets created immediately after somebody's death and placed on the altar during the wake and funeral.[17] They are typically made from unsealed beech wood. After the cremation, *uchi-ihai* are taken home and placed on the temporary altar along with the cremated remains until the interment ceremony. *Uchi-ihai* are then often dedicated to and cared for at a Buddhist temple.
- *No-ihai* (野位牌) are also temporary tablets, made from unsealed beech wood and placed on the gravesite after somebody's death. Upon the interment of cremated remains in the grave, they are usually ritually burnt or interred in the grave.
- *Hon-ihai* (本位牌) or true *ihai* are used after the 49-day ceremony as the ongoing receptacle for the deceased's spirit. They are typically made from black lacquered wood and decorated with elaborate carvings illuminated by gold leaf or paint. Modern *ihai* may be made from a broader range of materials and decorated with colourful, personalized designs. After the 49-day ceremony, they are stored within the household Buddhist altar.
- *Tera-ihai* (寺位牌) are given to the household's affiliated Buddhist temple, if such a relationship exists. They are stored in the temple *ihai-dō* (ihai hall), where they receive daily prayers from clergy.

When most people use the word *ihai*, they are referring to the *hon-ihai*, which function as the permanent receptacle of the deceased's spirit. Such *ihai* are generally around twelve centimetres high and three centimetres wide. Their size and design vary depending on the status of the deceased, the preferences of the family, and the size of the household altar. The front of *ihai* engraved with the individual's posthumous Buddhist name (戒名 *kaimyō*) and the back lists their given name, age, and the date of death. The inscriptions are made by hand, or more commonly today, by laser cutter. Occasionally, a married couple may share a single *ihai*, in which case the name of the still-living spouse may be inscribed in red ink. While temporary *ihai* are purchased from a funeral company immediately after somebody dies, *hon-ihai* are more expensive and elaborate. They are generally ordered from a Buddhist goods company before the 49-day ceremony. Cheaper *ihai*, mass produced overseas, are available only for as little as a few thousand yen, while hand-carved and hand-painted *ihai* can cost hundreds of thousands of yen.

Both *ihai* and these scrolls or books are typically enshrined within the household Buddhist altar or *butsudan* (Section 11.2.3). Several copies of *ihai* may be made and distributed among family members or enshrined in temples to ensure the dead are cared for and receive offerings regularly.[18] This reproduction does not appear to dilute the power of individual *ihai* to represent the dead. Depending on the teachings of different Buddhist schools, *ihai* are to be venerated for 33, 50, or 100 years, until the dead matures into a buddha or ancestor, and then can be disposed of via cremation at a temple. However, ethnographic research demonstrates that many households retain *ihai* within the Buddhist altar well beyond this timeline.[19] For those with multiple *ihai* to care for, the altar can become crowded and so a *kuridashi ihai* (繰り出し位牌) may be ordered, which contains multiple thin wooden strips engraved with each deceased's name.

11.2.3 Butsudan *(Domestic Buddhist Altar)*

Japanese families typically venerate the recently deceased alongside generations of ancestors within the home at the domestic Buddhist altar or *butsudan* (仏壇). *Butsudan* consist of a decorative double-door cabinet that enshrines a Buddhist icon, mortuary tablets, and an array of ritual goods and offerings. They are typically located in the head household of the patrilineal family line and are passed down between generations. In traditional Japanese homes, *butsudan* are positioned in a dedicated alcove in the formal *tatami* room but may be located in the living room for more contemporary floor plans.

The history of *butsudan* demonstrates the same hybridity and syncretism common to other aspects of Japanese religion and death culture. Three objects are identified as a predecessor for contemporary domestic Buddhist altars: 1) personal Buddhist halls (持仏堂 *jibutsudō*) commissioned by the aristocratic classes during the Heian period (794–1185); 2) shelves for mortuary tablets (位牌棚 *ihaidana*) which came to Japan with the spread of Confucianism; and 3) seasonal altars or shelves (魂棚 *tamadana*) for making offerings to the spirits of the dead as part of Japanese Shinto/folk traditions.[20] *Butsudan* became popular among common people during the Edo period, when the Tokugawa Shogunate mandated that households be affiliated with a Buddhist temple. Temples were required to certify that their patrons visited the temple frequently, owned prayer beads, and made regular offerings at a Buddhist icon.[21]

Traditional *butsudan* fall into two styles. The first, *kin butsudan* are decorated with Japanese lacquer and gold leaf. They are almost exclusively used by members of Pure Land Buddhism. The second, *karaki butsudan* are made from exotic woods like ebony, rosewood, or Yakushima cedar. A third style of *butsudan* gained popularity in Japan from the 1990s. Known variously as "modern", "city", or "furniture" *butsudan*, they are typically smaller and less ornate. Within the three general styles, *butsudan* further vary according to (1) the Buddhist school; (2) the regional artisan tradition; (3) the physical dimensions, often determined by their position in the home; (4) the design aesthetics of the maker or retailer; and (5) the personal preferences of the customer.

The interior of a *butsudan* has been described as a hierarchical structure with three tiers.[22] The top tier contains the main Buddhist icon (ご本尊 *gohonzon*) and attendant guardian deities and symbolizes the enlightened realm of the Buddha. The middle tier houses the mortuary tablets (位牌 *ihai*) and is considered the realm of the ancestors. The bottom tier, which contains food offerings and ritual instruments, symbolizes the mundane world of the living. Sasaki describes *butsudan* as thus producing a "religious cosmos" in miniature.[23] Beyond these tiers, surrounding the altar are various ritual instruments used to make offerings. *Butsudan* are a product of syncretic religious traditions and practices. The *butsudan* is where *hotoke* (ほとけ) is said to reside, but *hotoke* refers to the recently deceased, the ancestors, and to buddha simultaneously.

The *butsudan* is the locus of many rituals within the home. This includes informal daily observances and formal rituals for the recently deceased and ancestors. The *butsudan* is where people might place freshly cooked rice as an offering each morning, host formal celebrations for *Obon* (Section 11.3.2), burn incense and chant sutras, or introduce the ancestors to new children born into the family. Five offerings, known as the *gokū* (五供), are typically placed in front of the *butsudan*: incense, flowers, water (or tea), candles, and food. In addition, it is common for people to offer the favourite consumables of the deceased (such as sweets, alcohol, or tobacco). Gifts received by family members may be temporarily offered at the altar before being consumed by the (living) family.

The purchase of a *butsudan* is often a significant investment. *Butsudan* are inherited through the patrilineal family line, but newly bereaved families and branch families may purchase a new altar as part of the broader collection of memorial goods. *Butsudan* are available from specialty shops or through funeral homes. At *Obutsudan no Hasegawa*, one of the largest retail changes, altars range in cost from around ¥330,000 for a compact, desktop model to many tens of millions of yen for custom artisan-made designs.

11.2.4 Iei *(Memorial Portraits)*

Iei are formal portraits of the deceased. *Iei* have become an indispensable part of contemporary Japanese death rites, typically displayed on the funeral altar and carried with the remains to and from the crematorium[24]. After the funeral, they may be displayed in the home for several years or indeed, generations (see Figure 11.2). *Iei* tend to have a distinct style, similar to that of a passport photo, being a frontal head shot, cropped at chest level, against a neutral background.[25] Other contextualizing features of the photograph are usually digitally removed.

Figure 11.2 A *butsudan* in the style of Zen Buddhist school. Photograph by Hannah Gould (author), Hiroshima, 2022.

Printed *iei* tend to be around 20cm × 30cm and are surrounded by a white mounting board and a black frame. In recent years, personal photographs with more natural expressions and everyday clothing have begun to be used. The *iei* is often decorated with black and white ribbons during the funeral service. Unlike other memorial goods, *iei* can be prepared relatively quickly and cheaply by bereaved families via the local print shop or funeral company. Indeed, many elderly people will take professional portraits in preparation for their use as *iei* after their death.

Photo books began to be produced during the Meiji period (1868–1912), and portraits often appeared in the first pages of these books, accompanied by captions about the date and circumstances of the photograph.[26] Toward the late Meiji and early Taishō era (1912–1926), such captions were removed and *iei* began to be placed within black frames. This decontextualisation of the portraits signals their move from being snapshots of a biographical moment to becoming timeless icons of the dead.[27] Some people now place offerings before *iei* and personal photographs, as much as they would the Buddhist altar or mortuary tablets.[28]

11.2.5 Temoto Kuyōhin

A notable trend in Japanese funeral culture is the growing popularity of keepsakes for storing cremated remains within the home or on one's person, known collectively as *temoto kuyōhin* (手元供養品). These objects may be purchased together with or in lieu of a grave and Buddhist altar and may incorporate all or part of the cremated remains. This trend emerged in the mid-2000s,[29] driven at least partially by the expense and difficulty involved in acquiring a new grave. The practice of storing the dead in the home is a notable development, as it appears to run contrary to deep-rooted cultural taboos concerning the pollution (ケガレ *kegare*) generated by death, and in particular, human remains.[30]

There are a number of different classes of *temoto kuyōhin*. One popular type is a small urn or decorative container that holds a few grams of ash. It may be accompanied by a personal photograph of the dead and positioned in the home alongside flowers, incense, a bell and other offerings. There is a considerable 'DIY' element to many of these displays. Occasionally, the display is centred around a sentimental keepsake from the deceased, such as a wristwatch or wedding ring. Cremated remains may also be split between family members, or only a small amount retained at home, while the majority is interred at the grave or temple.

Another class of *temoto kuyōhin* is a type of jewellery, which often incorporates a receptacle with a few grams of ash. One Japanese company offers to compress human ash into a sapphire. Algordanza, a Swiss-based company, offers to compress ash into a single diamond. The latter process requires approximately 300 grams of ash to produce a one-carat diamond over the course of six months and costs up to ¥2.7 million. Yet another company, operating out of Aichi Prefecture, *Inori no Shinju*, transforms ash into pearls. Approximately 15 grams of human ash is finely ground and formed into balls, which are dried, cured, and inserted into oysters. The company raises the oysters at its farm over the course of a year, finally inviting the bereaved to help harvest the pearl and making fine jewellery.

11.2.6 Digital Memorials

Several digitally enabled memorial objects have been created, marketed, and sold in Japan. Predominantly, they incorporate digital devices and interfaces (e.g. screens and audio recordings) into traditional designs for altars, mortuary tablets, or jewellery. For example, the 'Fenestra', developed by Daisuke Uriu, combines a digital photo frame with a light-sensing candle interface and mirror.[31] There are also dedicated websites that offer on-demand live-streaming of *kuyō* services performed remotely at a temple, as well as phone apps and websites that reproduce, and in some cases gamify, the practice of ancestor veneration. However, to date, digitally enhanced memorial objects have not found widespread success in Japan.[32]

In Japan, the most popular social media services are LINE, Twitter, and Instagram.[33] In general, public memorial pages hosted on social media sites are an uncommon phenomenon, outside of the death of celebrities and major mass-death events. In the aftermath of the March 2011 earthquake, tsunami, and nuclear disaster, LINE became the key service for sharing updates about disaster-struck areas, searching for missing persons, and expressions of grief, both public and personal.[34]

11.3 Memorial Services

In Japan, depending on the particular religious affiliation and devotion of the household, memorial services or *hōji* (法事) may be held at set intervals of days, weeks, months, and years after a death. *Hōji* are occasions for feasting, listening to Buddhist teachings, and making offerings to the dead, buddha, and ancestors. They often involve inviting a priest to visit the household *butsudan*, the grave, or temple. Within most Buddhist traditions, they are aimed at praying for the welfare of the deceased. These services additionally serve the function of ensuring the dead are not lonely, and reassuring the living that they too will be cared for after death.[35]

11.3.1 Timing of Services

There is a complex timeline for services held after an individual's death, which corresponds with Buddhism, folk beliefs, and the Gregorian calendar. The reason behind the timing of these services is not necessarily widely understood by lay people,[36] and the practice and elaborateness of the ceremonies varies greatly. In Japan and many Buddhist countries, in the period of 49 days immediately following a death, the dead are said to reside in an intermediate state between this world and the next. According to some Buddhist teachings, the dead are judged by a deity, *Shinkōō*, for the merits of their deeds every seven days, seven times over. On the seventh day, the dead pass over the River Sanzu to the next life. On the 49th day, the final judgment is made by the deity *Taizanō*, who decides which of the six Buddhist realms (of gods, demi-gods, humans, animals, hungry ghosts, or hell denizens) the dead will be reborn into.

Memorial activities may also be held at intervals influenced by pre-Buddhist folk belief. These suggest that there are two aspects to an individual's soul, the wild *ara-mitama* (荒魂) and the refined *mitama* (和魂). Folk beliefs teach that the wild soul becomes a refined soul 33 years after a death, and many families thus hold services for this period. The year 33 is also significant within Buddhism, as the 13 buddhas of the afterlife are said to guide the spirit of the dead through this date. Other services are timed according to the Gregorian calendar, on the month or year anniversary of an individual's death. These services tend to conclude sometime between the 23rd and 50th anniversary of a death,[37] although they may continue for public figures.

11.3.2 Obon: Festival of the Ancestors

Obon (お盆) is a multi-day festival held during the summer in Japan with events to honour the recently deceased and ancestors. *Obon* is

Figure 11.3 A *bondana*, or temporary altar specially constructed for *obon*. Photograph by Shinya Yamada (author).

held at different times in different regions, either following the lunar calendar (July) or Gregorian calendar (August) between the 13th and 16th of the month. *Obon* coincides with and shares many features of 'hungry ghost' and 'grave sweeping' festivals throughout East Asia, as well as with autumn harvest and agricultural festivals.[38] The name *obon* derives from *urabon-e* (盂蘭盆会), the name of a Buddhist sutra composed in 6th-century China. It describes the Buddha's teachings on how to save the soul of the mother of Mokuren (one of the Buddha's disciples), who had fallen onto a path toward becoming a hungry ghost or demon posthumously.[39] By keeping Buddhist precepts and making various offerings, the petitioner was able to transfer the merits of their good labours to their mother and so changed her fate. *Urabon* ceremonies were sponsored by the Japanese imperial court as early as 606 CE.[40]

In Japan today, family remains the central emphasis of *Obon*. The festival is a public holiday and people travel back to their ancestral hometown to gather with family, hold feasts, and visit the grave. During *Obon*, the walls between this world and the next are said to be at their thinnest and the spirits of the dead return to the ancestral altar and grave. Special offerings are prepared to welcome the dead. An additional, temporary altar, known as the *bondana* or *shōryōdana* (盆棚・精霊棚) is erected and mortuary tablets are arranged on the top shelf. Offerings of fresh fruits and vegetables, flowers, seaweed and fish, bamboo, rice or rice cakes, and dumplings are arranged. Families (and especially children) also prepare horse or cow figurines (精霊馬) made from eggplants and cucumbers bisected by wooden chopsticks. These animals are said to aid the ancestors in their long journey home. A hanging scroll with the 13 buddhas that guide the dead in their passage through the afterworld may also be displayed.

The ancestral grave is cleaned and washed in preparation for *Obon* festivities. Families may light a welcoming fire (迎え火 *mukae-bi*) on the 13th to guide the ancestors home. Similarly, lanterns are a common decoration for the *Obon* altar or for outside the home. In Kyoto, five giant bonfires are lit in the mountains surrounding the city on the final day of *Obon* to send the spirits back to the after world. These fires, lit on the 15th or 16th, are known as *okuri-bi* (送り火).[41] Additionally, it is common to hold a *hōji* service for the dead on the first *obon* after somebody dies. White lanterns are commonly displayed on this occasion.

Special offerings or altars may also be created for hungry ghosts (餓鬼 *gaki*) who have died in unfortunate circumstances, or have been abandoned by the living. In some regions, *gakidana* (餓鬼棚) or *mizudana* (水棚) altars are set up outside and decorated with offerings of eggplant and cucumber cut into cubes and washed in rice, placed on a lotus leaf. While the *bondana* is for the ancestors, this altar is for the wandering dead.

Obon is also often accompanied by public festivals held at Buddhist temples or town centres. Most prominently, these festivals feature *bon odori*, a folk dance that is commonly performed around a central bamboo tower (*yagura*). Bon dances vary by region, and as participants often return to their hometowns during *Obon*, are an opportunity for the local community to reconnect. Originally intended to welcome and send off the spirits of the ancestors, bon dance has now become a form of community entertainment. Today, *bon odori* are held at festivals beyond Japan, for example, in North America, Hawaii, Brazil, and Malaysia, where there are large Japanese populations.

Another event on the Buddhist calendar is *higan* (彼岸), which takes place twice a year, across seven days, with the spring and autumn equinoxes acting as the middle day. These originated (and in some ways continue) as opportunities for intensive Buddhist practice in order to generate merit and evolved to incorporate veneration of the ancestral spirits. Unlike *Obon, higan* is only practiced in Japan.[42] Festivities at *higan* are often scaled-back versions of *Obon* celebrations, although it is more difficult for people to arrange to travel back to the ancestral home on these occasions.

Notes

1 Hannah Gould, *When Death Falls Apart: Making and Unmaking the Necromaterial Traditions of Contemporary Japan* (Chicago: Chicago University Press, 2023), 80–4.

2 Ikegami Yoshimasa 池上良正, "宗教学の研究課題としての「施餓鬼」," 駒沢大学文化 32 (2014): 69–94.

3 Tony Walter, "Communicating with the Dead," in *Encyclopedia of Death and the Human Experience,* eds. Clifton D. Bryant and Dennis L. Peck (Los Angeles: Sage Publications, 2009), 216–9.

4 Naitō Rieko 内藤理恵子, *現代日本の葬送文化* (東京: 岩田書院, 2013).

5 Angelika Kretschmer, "Mortuary rites for inanimate objects: The case of Hari *Kuyō*," *Japanese Journal of Religious Studies* 27, no. 3/4 (2000): 379–404.

6 Jennifer Robertson, "Robot reincarnation: Rubbish, artefacts, and mortuary rituals," in *Consuming life in post-bubble Japan: A transdisciplinary perspective*, eds. Katarzyna J. Cwiertka and Ewa Machotka (Amsterdam: Amsterdam University Press, 2018).

7 Mayumi Itoh, *The Japanese culture of mourning whales: Whale graves and memorial monuments in Japan* (Princeton: Palgrave MacMillan, 2018).

8 Pamela J. Asquith, "The monkey memorial service of Japanese primatologists," in *Japanese culture and behaviour: Selected readings*, eds. Takie Sugiyama Lebra and William P. Lebra (Honolulu: University of Hawai'i Press, 1986), 29–32.

9 Barbara Ambros, *Bones of contention: Animals and religion in contemporary Japan* (Honolulu: University of Hawai'i Press, 2012).

10 Matsuzaki Kenzō 松崎憲三, "動植物の供養覚書:供養碑建立習俗をめぐって," in *民俗的世界の探求*, ed. Kamata Hisako Sensei Koki Kinenronshū Hensan Iinkai 鎌田久子先生古稀記念論集編纂委員会, (東京: 慶友社 1996).

11 Ōsaki Tomoko 大崎智子, "ハサミ供養をめぐって：東京都港区芝増上寺," 民具祭り 30, no. 1 (1997): 14–24.

12 Helen Hardcare, *Marketing the menacing fetus in Japan* (Berkeley: University of California Press, 1997); William R. LaFleur, *Liquid life: Abortion and Buddhism in Japan* (Princeton: Princeton University Press, 1992).

13 Less commonly, 霊牌 *reihai*.

14 Fabio Rambelli, "Home Buddhas: Historical processes and modes of representation of the sacred in the Japanese Buddhist family altar (butsudan)," *Japanese Religions* 35, nos. 1–2 (2010): 75; Joshua A. Irizarry, "Signs of life: Grounding the transcendent in Japanese memorial objects," *Signs and Society* 2, no. 1 (2014): S160–S187.

15 Hirayama Toshijirō 平山敏治郎, "神棚と仏壇," 史林 32, no. 2 (1949): 65.

16 Yanagita Kunio 柳田國男, *先祖の話* (東京: 筑摩書房, 1946); Hirayama 平山, "神棚と仏壇," 53; Himon'ya Hajime 碑文谷創, 葬儀概論 四訂版 (東京: 葬祭ディレクター技能審査協会, 2017), 184.

17 Himonya 碑文谷, 葬儀概論 四訂版, 184.

18 Irizarry, "Signs of life," 165.

19 Robert John Smith, *Ancestor worship in contemporary Japan* (Stanford: Stanford University Press, 1974).

20 Butsuji kōdinētā shikaku shinsa kyōkai 仏事コーディネーター資格審査協会, ed., *仏壇仏具ガイダンス：よりよい仏壇店を目指して*, 4th ed. (東京: 全日本宗教用具協同組合, 2015), 176.

21 Fabio Rambelli, *Buddhist materiality* (Stanford: Stanford University Press, 2007), 73.

22 Gorai Shigeru 五来重, 日本人の死生観 (東京: 講談社, 1994); Sasaki Kōkan 佐々木宏幹, *仏と霊の人類学：仏教文化の深層構造* (東京: 春秋社, 1993); Rambelli, *Buddhist materiality*.

23 Sasaki 佐々木, *仏と霊の人類学*, 27–34.

24 Yamada Shinya 山田慎也, *現代日本の死と葬儀* (東京: 東京大学出版会, 2007).

25 Irizarry, "Signs of life," 162.

26 Yamada Shinya 山田慎也 "遺影と死者の人格：葬儀写真集における肖像写真の扱いを通して," 国立歴史民俗博物館研究報告 169 (2011): 137–66.

27 Ibid, 162; 139.

28 Suzuki Iwayumi, "Beyond ancestor worship: Continued relationship with significant others," in *Death and dying in contemporary Japan*, ed. Hikaru Suzuki (London: Routledge, 2013).

29 Naitō 内藤, *現代日本の葬送文化*, 203–5.

30 Hikaru Suzuki, The Price of Death: The Funeral Industry in Contemporary Japan (Stanford: Stanford University Press, 2000); Shintani Takanori 新谷尚紀, 日本人と葬儀 (東京: 紀伊國屋, 1992).

31 Daisuke Uriu and William Odom, "Designing for Domestic Memorialization and Remembrance: A Field Study of Fenestra in Japan," in *Proceedings of the 2016 CHI Conference on Human Factors in Computing Systems (CHI '16)* (2016): 5945–57.

32 Hannah Gould, Tamara Kohn and Martin Gibbs, "Uploading the ancestors: Experiments with digital Buddhist altars in contemporary Japan," *Death Studies* 43, no. 7 (2019): 456–65.

33 We Are Social, *Digital 2023 Global Overview Report*, accessed December 20, 2023, https://wearesocial.com/jp/blog/2023/01/digital-2023/. These statistics do not include YouTube.

34 Larissa Hjorth, "The place of data: Mobile media, loss and data in life, death and afterlife," *Memory Studies* 14, no. 3 (2021): 592.

35 Tanaka Jirō 田中治郎, supervised by Yamaori Tetsuo 山折哲雄, 面白い ほどよくわかる日本の宗教 (東京：日本文芸社, 2005), 288.

36 Ibid, 288–90.

37 Ibid, 291.

38 Nara Yasuaki奈良康明, ed., 日本の仏教を知る事典 (東京: 東京書籍), 303.

39 Ibid.

40 The Nihon Shoki (日本書紀) or 'Chronicle of Japan' is the second oldest extant work of classical Japanese history, dated to 720 AD.

41 Tanaka 田中, 面白いほどよくわかる日本の宗教, 296.

42 Nara, 日本の仏教を知る事典, 298.

12 Conservation

12.1 Cemetery Conservation

Compared to western societies such as the UK, in Japan, the recognition of the historical and cultural value of cemeteries and a movement toward their preservation is less advanced. One reason for this is that since the establishment of the basic cemetery administrative framework in the 19th century, it has been broadly accepted that the grave is a symbol of household, and thus the ongoing management of graves is the responsibility of that household, not the community or state. It remains common for graves to be used by multiple generations of a family and there is a strong sense that graves are essentially private property. Therefore, even historical headstones are left to the care of relatives. Old graves may be disposed of or set aside to make way for a new gravestone, or the grave itself may be abolished, as per the living relatives' desires.

Once cemeteries reach capacity, there is no guarantee that graves will be permanently preserved. As described in Chapter 10, cemetery management is legally empowered to clear neglected graves to make more space and users are also encouraged to return their grave plot if they no longer need it. As such, cemetery space in Japan has a regular turn-over for new users. For example, although the Aoyama Cemetery in Tokyo was created in 1872 and is one of the oldest continuing cemeteries in Japan, it is still an active cemetery accepting new interments, because cemetery management actively promotes the clearance of neglected graves.

There are few examples of community activities or 'friends' groups' that advocate to protect local cemeteries as heritage sites. However, as will be discussed below, there are national conservation

DOI: 10.4324/9781003451914-12

initiatives for the tombs of emperors, feudal lords, and other important figures (Section 12.2). Further, in recent years, there has emerged a movement to use cemeteries to protect the natural environment via strategic tree burials (Section 12.3).

12.2 Notable Protected Tombs

12.2.1 *Emperors' Mausoleums (*Ryōbo*)*

In Japan, the mausoleums of all successive emperors, from the first and legendary Emperor Jinmu (said to have lived in 6th century BC) to the 124th Emperor Shōwa, who died in the post-war period, are identified, maintained, and protected by the state. However, these mausolea are not protected for their cultural, historical, or aesthetic value, but rather, as part of the Imperial household system. All imperial mausolea are cared for by the Imperial Household Agency (*Kunaichō*), a Cabinet agency that has jurisdiction over the affairs of the imperial household and emperors. The Agency currently manages 188 mausolea, which are those of the Emperor, Empress, Empress Dowager, and Grand Empress Dowager; 555 graves of other members of the imperial family; 42 important sites which are equivalent to mausoleums, such as mounds holding bone or ash; 68 pagodas enshrining relics such as hair, teeth, and nails; and 46 additional sites where the interred person cannot be identified, but the site is likely to be a mausoleum.[1] These mausolea are not simply graves, where the dead are interred, but are regarded as "sanctuaries", where commercialisation and political exploitation is prohibited. Each location[2] is set up as a sacred place worthy of public remembrance and veneration. For example, many mausolea are designed with burial mounds surrounded by evergreen trees and are maintained as solemn landscapes with *torii* gates (found at the entrance to Shinto shrines), lanterns, and paths for worshippers. Although mausolea placed under state control thus enjoy generous protection, this is not necessarily due to their value as cultural heritage. Rather, many imperial graves were newly created as a product of the modern emperor system, and their historic value is subordinate to their status as sanctuaries.

The process of identifying buried persons in mausolea using historical sources has been conducted since the Edo period (1603–1868), but it was not until after the Meiji Restoration of 1868 that this became a fully fledged process. The Meiji Government established a restorative political system centred on the supremacy of the Emperor, and so tried to promulgate the image of a continuous imperial family line stretching back to ancient times. In order to demonstrate the legitimacy of the imperial family both domestically and internationally, the mythical Emperor Jinmu was designated as the founder of the imperial household, and the mausolea of subsequent emperors were identified and repaired. However, because this work was done hastily, based mainly on mythological documents such as the *Kojiki* and *Nihonshoki*, inscriptions, and oral traditions, the real identity of buried persons at some designated mausolea has been questioned by current scholarship.[3]

Most imperials mausoleums are Takatsuka-style tumuls (a mound of earth and stone raised over a grave). However, due to the influence of Buddhism, which has enjoyed a close relationship with the imperial household since its introduction, there are also Buddhist-style mausoleums at Sennyūji Temple in Kyoto, the imperial family's temple. Perhaps the most famous emperor's mausoleum in Japan today is the Daisenryō-kofun in Sakai, Osaka (Figure 12.1). This is Japan's largest forward-rectangular burial mound, measuring 840 metres in length including the moat and covering an area of 464,000 square metres. This mausoleum is administered by the Imperial Household Agency as the grave of emperor Nintoku, the 16th Emperor of Japan. It was recognised as a UNESCO World Heritage Site in 2019.

The most recent imperial mausoleum is that of Emperor Shōwa, who died in 1989, which stands alongside the mausolea of Emperor and Empress Taishō, and Empress Shōwa, at the Musashi-ryō grave site in Hachiōji, Tokyo. The burial rites of modern emperors accompany a large-scale ceremony.[4] However, in 2013, the Imperial Household Agency announced that the 125th Emperor (now Emperor Emeritus, Akihito) and Empress would be cremated instead of buried, in accordance with the Emperor's wish to support simplified funeral rites.

Although anyone, not just members of the royal family, can visit the mausolea, opportunities for excavation and other research and investigation are severely restricted due to their designation as sacred areas. However, a path is gradually opening up for these sites to further open to the public, partly due to the aforementioned recognition of Taisenryō-kofun as a World Cultural Heritage Site.

Figure 12.1 The distinctive shape and massive scale of kofun tombs is evident in this aerial photograph of the Mozu Tombs Cluster in Sakai, Osaka Prefecture. Reproduced freely from the Geospatial Information Authority of Japan.

12.2.2 Daimyō *Graves (*Daimyō-bo*)*

It was only in the late Edo period (c. 1750) that many people in Japan, including ordinary people, began to erect formal graves. Accordingly, many gravestones from this early modern period remain today. However, these gravestones have not been valued in historical research until recently. The Edo period had one of the highest literacy rates in the world and left behind an abundance of written material, and as such, there has been limited need to utilise graves as historical sources. Furthermore, these graves are still privately managed by relatives. In recent years, however, archaeological research into early modern graves has progressed, and people have begun to appreciate the historical and cultural value of the graves of powerful warrior families, especially those known as feudal lords or *daimyō,* who governed estates and controlled many retainers. As a result, there are now graves of *daimyō* (*daimyo-bo*) that are subject to protection as nationally designated cultural heritage under the Act on Protection of Cultural Properties (文化財保護法).

A characteristic feature of early modern *daimyō* graves is that they are extremely large in size, both in terms of gravesites and headstones. This is because, under the Tokugawa clan-based shogunate system, *daimyō* graves were built to demonstrate the legitimacy of each family's power. Within a complex, each interment was also ordered by design, size, and layout in accordance with their status and position, making these sites a powerful medium for expressing the order of succession and power over time.[5] For example, Tokugawa Ieyasu, who founded the Edo Shogunate, is enshrined at the UNESCO World Heritage-listed Nikko Toshogu Shrine, which has a magnificent gate and various shrines. The pagoda containing his grave is located deep within the precinct. It was built on an octagonal five-storey stone base with three bronze steps and is about five metres high. A hall for worshipping at the pagoda has also been built. Most of the structures, including the grave, are registered as national important cultural assets.

Daimyō graves that have recently been registered as nationally designated cultural properties include the Maeda family graveyard of the Kaga domain lord in Ishikawa and Toyama prefectures (registered in 2009), and the Yamauchi family graveyard of the Tosa domain lord in Kochi prefecture (registered in 2016). The grave of the second lord Maeda Toshinaga, located in Takaoka City, Toyama Prefecture, is a square plot measuring approximately 180 metres on each side and is one of the largest private graves of a feudal lord in Japan. A stone pagoda measuring over five metres is erected on a three-storey platform in the centre of the gravesite, which is surrounded by a double moat. The Yamauchi family graveyard in Kochi Prefecture also provides insight into the social status ladder of the time through its grave system, with the grave of the first feudal lord Kazutoyo at the topmost level, the graves of successive lords at the middle level and the graves of their children at the lowest level. These graveyards are valued for their design, well-preserved condition, and for being valuable artifacts that provide insight into the burial system under the shogunate.[6]

12.3 Cemeteries as Nature Preserves

In Japan, cemeteries have long been thought of as places dedicated to interring the dead and performing the associated rituals. This situation has begun to change in recent years, however, via the emergence of a movement to utilise cemeteries as places for nature conservation. As described in Section 10.3.4, an alternative interment method known as tree burial was first proposed in Japan in 1999 and has spread across the country since. The original founder of tree burial, Chisaka Genpō, a Buddhist priest of Iwate Prefecture, proposed the integration of interment and forest conservation by burying cremated remains directly in the ground and planting a tree as a grave marker instead of a headstone. He aimed to protect the natural landscape and ecosystem of his local area, and to encourage temple activities that used these natural resources.[7] His innovation opened up the possibility of cemeteries as places dedicated to the protection of the natural environment.

However, given the enormous amount of labour and expertise required to create and sustain a cemetery like Chisaka proposed, the original form of tree burial has not spread widely. Today, the most common form of tree burial is a space is created in a corner of an existing cemetery, with remains interred underneath memorial trees. However, there is now renewed interest in seeing Chisaka's original vision to fruition. One such cemetery is 'Mori no Boen' or the Forest Cemetery, run by the Ecosystem Conservation Society Japan (日本生態系協会). The society is an environmental NGO established in 1992 to protect and restore healthy ecosystems for the purpose of sustainable community development, and its main activities include publicity and environmental education, research and surveys, and national trust projects.[8] In Japan, as cemetery management agencies are strictly restricted and cemeteries are largely managed by local authorities or Buddhist temples, it is extremely rare for an environmental organisation to establish a cemetery. The Ecosystem Conservation Society Japan inspected and gathered information about not only on the original Japanese tree burial site in Iwate but also on cemeteries in the UK, the USA, South Korea, Germany, and other countries, where practices similar to tree burial, like natural burial, are popular. They finally purchased land in Chiba Prefecture and opened the Forest Cemetery in 2016. As with other tree burial sites, the remains are buried in the soil and trees are planted as grave markers, but the Forest Cemetery is unique in that it will be completely restored to a forest 50 years after its opening. After 50 years the frequency of mowing will be gradually reduced, and no burial plots will be reused so that the site can be conserved as forest. Rather than selling graves, the cemetery is based on the model of a National Trust that will restore and preserve the site using contractors' fees.[9] Other examples of this movement include "Komorebi to Hoshi no Sato" in Osaka Prefecture, which is based on German-style tree burials[10] and the "Return to Nature" service practiced at Mt Myōken in Osaka. The latter has registered a trademark under the Junkan-sō (循環葬), or 'Circulation Burial', clearly differentiating it from conventional tree burial.[11]

Notes

1 Imperial Household Agency 宮内庁, 陵墓, accessed November 7, 2023, www.kunaicho.go.jp/about/shisetsu/others/ryobo.html.
2 A full list of locations can be found at www.kunaicho.go.jp/ryobo/index.html.
3 Takagi Hiroshi 高木博志, 陵墓と文化財の近代 (東京: 山川出版社, 2010).
4 Edmund T. Gilday, "Bodies of Evidence: Imperial Funeral Rites and the Meiji Restoration," *Japanese Journal of Religious Studies* 27, no. 3/4 (2000): 273–96; Inoue Makoto 井上亮, 天皇と葬儀:日本人の死生観 (東京:新潮社, 2000).

  It was not until the Meiji period that the earth burial of emperors became customary. Although, before that that time, it was not uncommon for emperors to be cremated, partly due to Buddhist influence. The practice of burying emperors was originally established in an attempt to remove Buddhist elements from the imperial rituals.
5 Sekine Tatsuhito 関根達人, 墓が語る江戸時代: 大名・庶民の墓事情 (東京: 吉川弘文館, 2018).
6 Agency for Cultural Affairs 文化庁, 国指定文化財等データベース, accessed June 11, 2024, https://kunishitei.bunka.go.jp/bsys/index.
7 Sébastien Penmellen Boret, *Japanese Tree Burial: Ecology, Kinship and the Culture of Death* (London: Routledge, 2014).
8 Ecosystem Conservation Society-Japan 公益財団法人日本生態系協会, "About Us," accessed June 11, 2024, https://www.ecosys.or.jp/aboutus/english/index.html.
9 Uchida Aki 内田安紀, "樹木葬墓地が拓く公益的な墓地活用の可能性," 冠婚葬祭総合研究所報告書(2018), 62–65.
10 Osaka Hokusetsu Reien 大阪北摂霊園, "木もれびと星の里," accessed June 11, 2024, https://jyumoku.toshiseibi.org/.
11 At Forest Inc., "Return to Nature," accessed June 11, 2024, https://returntonature.jp/.

Index

For Product Safety Concerns and Information please contact our EU
representative GPSR@taylorandfrancis.com
Taylor & Francis Verlag GmbH, Kaufingerstraße 24, 80331 München, Germany

www.ingramcontent.com/pod-product-compliance
Ingram Content Group UK Ltd.
Pitfield, Milton Keynes, MK11 3LW, UK
UKHW021820240425
457818UK00001B/1